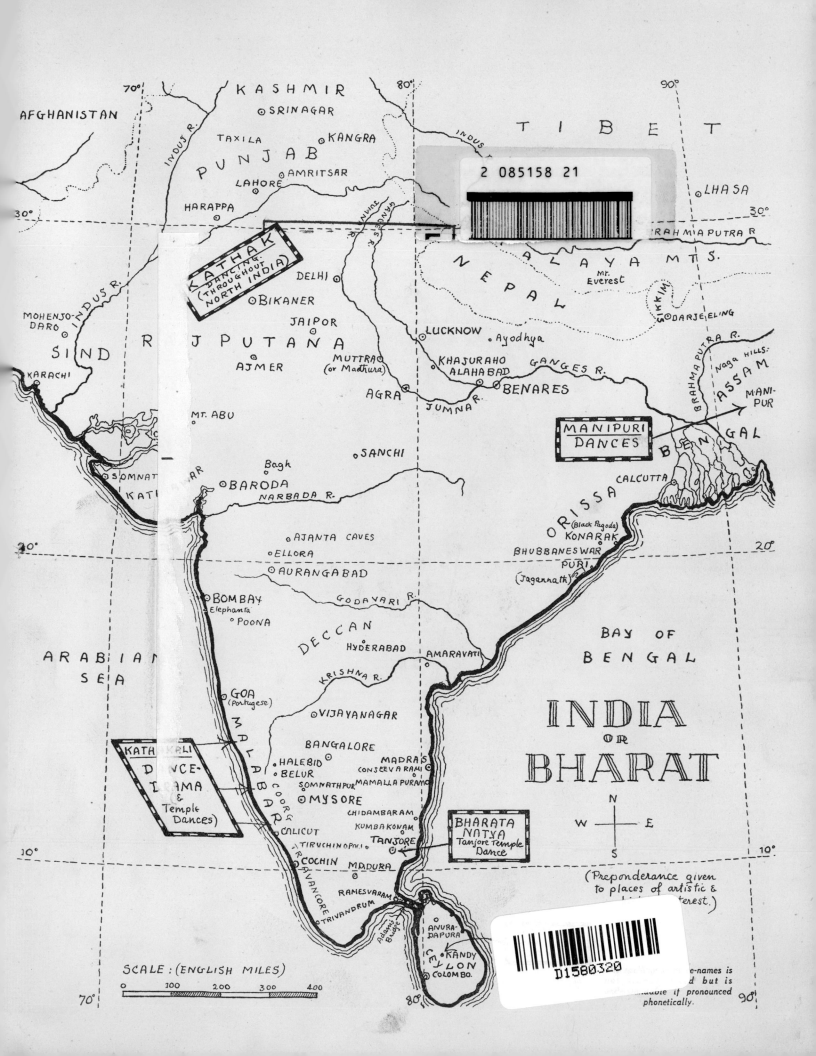

RAM GOPAL IN BELUR TEMPLE, MYSORE STATE

DYANA

Lokānāhuya-sarbān-damarukaninādai-ghora-sansarā-magnān
Datwāvitim-dayālu-pranatavayaharam-kuncitam-pād-padmam
Udhrityedam-bimukterayanamiti-karāddarsayan-pratyayaratham
Bivrad-bahnim-savāyām kalyati natanam ya-sa-pāyānnateśa.

Invocation to Siva

*Calling by the beat of the drum all persons engrossed in worldly affairs, the kind-hearted
One who destroys all fear of the meek and gives them reassurance, and points by his hand
to his upraised lotus-foot (bent at the knee) as the refuge of salvation and also carries the
fire and who dances in the assembly hall (universe), let that Lord of the Dance protect us.*

CLASSICAL DANCES AND COSTUMES OF INDIA

BY

KAY AMBROSE

INTRODUCTION BY

RAM GOPAL

FOREWORD BY
ARNOLD HASKELL

53 ILLUSTRATIONS FROM PHOTOGRAPHS
AND MANY DRAWINGS BY THE AUTHOR

GANESHA DANCING

ADAM AND CHARLES BLACK
4, 5 AND 6 SOHO SQUARE LONDON, W.1

FIRST PUBLISHED 1950
A. & C. BLACK LTD
4, 5 & 6 SOHO SQUARE, LONDON, W.1

This volume is inscribed to

RAM GOPAL

through whose art the glorious past of India
has come to life once more
and whose incomparable performance has
set a new standard for the future

PRINTED BY THE WHITEFRIARS PRESS LIMITED LONDON AND TONBRIDGE

CONTENTS

PART I

PART II

LIST OF PLATES

The author's grateful thanks are due to the photographers whose work is reproduced in this book. Most of the photographs come from Ram Gopal's personal scrap-book and unfortunately many of the photographers' names have become obliterated through being pasted in an album. Acknowledgment is made to the photographer wherever his name is known, and full acknowledgment will be made to the others in future editions of this book if their names become known.

INDIAN DANCE IN THE BALLET: from contemporary portraits.

Marie TAGLIONI in "LA BAYADÈRE," circa 1830. (Based on devadasi)

Vaslav NIJINSKY in "LE DIEU BLEU" (THE BLUE GOD) 1912. (Based on Krishna)

Anna PAVLOVA in "LA BAYADÈRE", 1906. (based on North Indian bayadère)

Carlotta GRISI and Lucien PETIPA, "LA PERI," 1844

The Sage,
Bharata Muni
writing the
Natya Sastras.
(After an Indian
lithograph.)

INTRODUCTION

By Ram Gopal

I MET Kay Ambrose in 1939 during my first visit to London's theatreland. Miss Ambrose was at the beginning of her career as an author and artist of dancing and particularly Russian ballet and was preparing her first work with Arnold Haskell, and she came backstage at the Aldwych Theatre to make sketches of my performance and gather information for her book, and thus we met.

I answered Miss Ambrose's questions as simply as I could and we soon became good friends. I told her she ought to study the Indian dance with a view to preparing a book on the subject, as she seemed to catch movement with ease and accuracy. On my next visit to London less than a year later, the Vaudeville Theatre in 1940, there was Miss Ambrose with an enormous sketch-book and quantities of pencils, energy and determination to learn all she could. She watched me practise, attacked all Indian subject-matter including our music, and accompanied my little group and myself during our small tour of England immediately after our stay in London. Then the war-clouds which had been gathering burst, my musicians grew anxious and I had to return to India. Miss Ambrose sent me a copy of the *Balletomane's Sketchbook*, her book with Haskell, and the *critiques* which said that the drawings of Indian dancing were the best. Here is a letter I wrote to her in 1942.

5

Bangalore, February, 1942.

MY DEAR KAY,

Your letter reached me safely and I am glad you got my parcel of books. If you absorb them thoroughly, and continue to refresh your memory of the Indian dance in the way I suggested, by visiting the British Museum's stock of sculptures and paintings, you'll find that later on when you can visit India you will understand the Indian dance far more readily. And keep your eyes open in London—you'll be surprised how many junk-shops have real treasures of Indian art in them, brought over by English people who learned to love and understand our Indian expression of beauty. (I don't mean you to *buy* them, only to *look* at them!)

I often think of the ballets I saw in Europe and the lovely long, straight lines of the dancers. Carry on with your studies of the ballet and do lots of books. I know that ballet is in its infancy compared with our ancient dances over here, but it's a lusty infant and by far the best medium of dancing I saw in the West, and there is no doubt that whereas our dancers could teach yours a good deal, yet in India we have everything to learn from you concerning organisation and stage presentation. I have a strong feeling that through ballet, dancing is going to become a part of everyday life in the West as well as the East—and I bet you A. L. H.* will have a good deal to do with that transformation; he was telling me his ideas of a National ballet in England when we met in Bournemouth, and I told him we should have something on the same lines over here in India.

You remember I told you the story of "Bharata Natya," the ancient dance of the bayadères that I'm sure Pavlova was seeking and never found because everyone in India told her that it had died out? And I showed you some of the movements? Well, I am going to put in some really high-pressure work with Meenakshi Sundaram Pillai. Krishna Iyer, the greatest critic and writer of B. Natya over here says that some of the dances and movements can be best performed by men, and Meenakshi S. is the greatest teacher of all in the vigorous style. So Krishna Iyer and I are going to Tanjore together soon and I'm going to work like mad, live in a hut and dance till I drop on Meenakshi S.'s mud classroom floor, until he says I am perfectly trained. If only those ballet-dancers of yours could see our classrooms in India, how they would appreciate their mirrors, bars and nice level wooden floors!

As soon as possible I will come back to England and bring a real company with me this time. You'll be able to join my tours and then come to India with me, and see for yourself the things I've described to you, done my best to show you and told you how to read up and study on your own. I always make my dancers *study* the dance as well as practise it, and you as a writer and artist should study far, far more than they do.

So you work hard and I'll work hard, and we'll see what we can do about this book between us. But you MUST see the dance in its proper setting here in India first. Just you wait till you see Balasaraswathi—I'll ask her to dance specially for you. I have the instinct that this poor old world is going to need all the spiritual consolation the real Indian dance can give, and the sooner the better.

Incidentally I enclose a taste of what you'll see one day soon—some photos of

* Arnold L. Haskell.

my recent performance in Belur Temple in Mysore State. The floor was specially made for dancing, and the last person to dance on it did so nearly 2,000 years ago. . . .

.   .   .   .

All that remains to be said is that in due course I returned to London with my company and found Londoners, along with the rest of the world, more than ready to welcome the Indian dance and Miss Ambrose, now well-versed in Indian mythology and literature, ready and equipped to deal with the realities of authorship. I started my second European tour with a season at London's Princes Theatre in December, 1947, with Miss Ambrose in attendance, making copious notes and sketches. As I had foreseen, she accompanied me on my European tour, working furiously all the time, and finally returned with me to India and completed her Indian dance education by meeting all the old great dance-masters, their prize pupils, and attending performances of every kind including classes, rehearsals, village festivals and many other occasions which included dancing of any sort.

Following her method of studying the ballet, which she learned to perform herself so that she could sketch and describe the movements with understanding and accuracy, she has studied the rudiments of Indian dancing in the same spirit and achieved the same results; in other words her sketches in this book are accurate to a degree hitherto unknown in any country, and they conserve at the same time a strong sense of movement which is usually lacking in purely diagrammatic drawings.

I can recommend this book unconditionally to any dance-lover or student, and am convinced that in India it will become the treasured possession of every cultivated family, and the indispensable text-book of every Indian dancer.

It is the first book of its kind ever to appear in print.

RAM GOPAL

London, 1950

From a
JAIN PAINTING, 15ᵀᴴ CENTURY: (DANCING
ON A NEEDLE) NOTE COSTUME, PLAIT, ETC.

FOREWORD

I am convinced that Kay Ambrose has asked me to write a preface to her book because she knows that I know nothing about Indian dancing. I enjoy it immensely and that is important, but the maximum enjoyment only comes with real understanding. Therefore she has written this book for me. It is clear, vivid, enthusiastic and contains some of her finest work as an artist. It is going to add enormously to the enjoyment of Indian dancing. I may even be able to borrow some of her knowledge and get away with a reputation as a pundit. Many a reputation has been founded on less.

The greatest hindrance to the pure enjoyment of the Indian, or for that matter the Spanish, dance lies in the use, often by the spurious critic, of the word *authentic*. I have seen dancing in India and I realise that it cannot be transferred to the Western stage without a process of translation. The real thing dumped on one of our stages would be intolerable, it would in fact be unreal. Authenticity is a word that needs amplification. Authenticity of spirit is the thing that counts. Ballet people have often misunderstood that when they have taken *Giselle*, *Swan Lake* or *Les Sylphides* and set them down in some vast sports arena. I feel that Ram Gopal has thoroughly understood this point. Some experts may tell me that he has taken great liberties with the Indian classical dance. Of course he has, because he knows what our stage demands. But the essential spirit remains. Ram Gopal is a highly conscious artist and this translation is a conscious process. It works in practice and only when we know everything can we differ with him on points of detail. Like Kay Ambrose I feel strongly that we must steer a clear path between semi-punditry and the intoxication of the oriental bazaar so very prevalent with those who see in every Indian a highly spiritual being. This book will help enormously in such clear thinking.

I would like to close on a personal note. Many years ago a common friend sent me a letter about Kay Ambrose. She was a ballet enthusiast and would like to sketch dancers. Of course I ignored it. Practically everyone seems to be a ballet enthusiast and wishes to sketch dancers. Then she rang me up and asked to see me. She had an attractive voice and I consented. I am glad that she had an attractive voice.

ARNOLD L. HASKELL

LONDON, 1950.

PREFACE

EXPLANATION FOR THE READER

It is both customary and sensible to preface a book on dancing with a clear and brief description of the distinguishing features of the dance with which the book deals. In this case it should be explained without further ado that the four main schools of classical Indian dancing do not lend themselves easily to either brevity or clarity, which is why the rarely-available books on even one style of Indian dancing usually have the effect of confusing instead of enlightening the reader.

Here I have done my best to prepare a book in which the four schools are treated with the greatest possible clarity and economy, and in their relation to one another. It must be observed that each separate school has a tradition of several thousand years, and that the history of each one is inextricably involved with the tumultuous and colourful history of the vast sub-continent of India. The main problem has been how to give clear and brief information concerning such a confused and romantic subject as that of the dances of India; if one attempted to include everything, the length of the work would obliterate its main object; yet if one left out those features relating to religion, mythology, art, environment and foreign conquests, which have made the dance what it is, one would risk being guilty of painting only half a picture.

So I have evolved a policy to solve this difficulty. There are many excellent books available concerning Indian art, philosophy, history and so forth, and in most of them are references to other books. I have added a small bibliography at the end of this volume containing a list of the most readily understandable works, contented myself with giving only the barest and most necessary outlines of Indian history that I can command, and have made sketches of just those bronzes, sculptures, murals and miniatures which are indispensable to an under-standing of the dance—and which will give the reader an obvious clue as to how he may continue to study the Indian dance on his own account. I have tried to avoid difficult words and names wherever possible; the reader can accustom himself to such terms at his leisure, with the aid of the works described.

RAM GOPAL

In the year 1939 I had seen various performances described as Indian dancing, and these performances affected me so that I had to be dragged by discerning friends to see the performance of Ram Gopal. I knew that there had been a great and ancient classical dance-tradition in India, but after seeing the only available demonstrations of Indian dancing in London I had been forced to the conclusion that Anna Pavlova's Indian informants were quite right when they told her the classical styles were no more. I was prepared to admit that some of the dancers I had seen were genuinely Indian, but the classical style I had hoped to see was not in evidence.

An ancient classical dance-style has a force which is immediately perceptible in the theatre, and contrary to "intellectual" belief it almost invariably attracts the general public. In the same way that people are consciously attracted to any film which features the incomparable Greta Garbo—because they know that in her performance they are sure of a certain standard of entertainment—so they are attracted, but instinctively this time, by a great classical dance-style. They saw Ram Gopal, and even before he had the chance of explaining in public that his country's classical dances had survived, as he did on his return to Europe in 1947, they knew that this must be so from his dances, and flocked to admire and learn. Accompanied by raving friends, and braced against possible disillusionment, I went to a performance at the Aldwych Theatre in 1939.

Ram Gopal was then a youth who had even by that time been round the world and earned considerable fame, with solo performances at first and then the little group and orchestra which we saw at the Aldwych. Physically a stripling, the maturity of his dancing was an absolute indication that here, very much alive, was the classical dance of India, which had been thought to be extinct. I lost no time in making the acquaintance of the boy Ram Gopal, and thus my education in Indian dancing began.

Even the most unobservant reader, on glancing through these pages must be conscious that this book *is* Ram Gopal. I have used his library, his collection of arts and antiques, I have been led by him through the nerve-centres of the dance in India (and these are often remote and well-hidden). Ram Gopal has tirelessly performed dance-sequences over and over again, and by virtue of his extreme patience appears in the large majority of the technical sketches, all of which he corrected himself. I should like to place on record that even as the present renaissance and prosperity of the Indian dance in India as in the Western hemisphere is due to the faith, courage and unremitting labours of Ram Gopal, so the very existence and vitality of this book are due to him; whereas the mistakes (and there must be quite a number by the very character of the work) are mine, the lucky illuminator and scribe.

A SUMMARY OF THE VARIOUS DANCE-STYLES

The four main schools of Indian dancing as accepted to-day are:

1. *BHARATA NATYA(M)*, or *Devadasiattam*, the courtesan temple-dance of Tanjore, South India.

2. *KATHAKALI*, the dance-drama of Malabar, also in the South.

3. *KATHAK*, the whirling dance of the North.

4. *MANIPURI*, the rhythmical, swaying, sinuous and sometimes powerful dance of Manipur in the state of Assam, in the North-East.

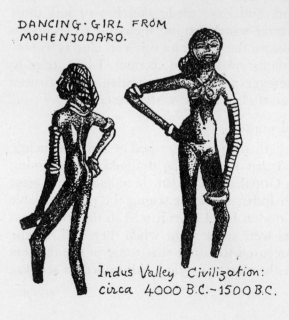

DANCING·GIRL FROM MOHENJODARO.

Indus Valley Civilization: circa 4000 B.C.~1500 B.C.

Bharata's *Natya Sastra*, the ancient treatise on drama, music and dancing, is the most complete Sanskrit work which remains to us in the great Sanskrit centres of India. All the fragmentary dance-dramas and styles existing to-day in both the South and the North of India are to a certain extent linked to this monumental treatise so clearly laid out in the *Sastra*, which is described more clearly later on.

All the four dance-styles as mentioned above are incomplete aspects of the *Natya Sastra*. Many movements of gesture, expression and choreography have been lost through antiquity. The *gurus* or masters of the Indian dance to-day all have their own personal opinions and views concerning the original dance. For instance, the *Kathakali* dance-drama of Malabar has developed contrary to some of the precepts of the *Sastra* and is condemned by many Sanskrit professors as a result; but the deviations are carefully considered and with a local purpose and may therefore be considered healthy. In dancing, it is lack of principles of any kind, or meaningless adherence to pedantic traditions, which cause damage and limitation.

The four main schools are dealt with in turn in the course of this book. I believe that even the casual reader, in giving a cursory glance to the drawings, will get a strong impression of the essential precision with governs Indian dancing, and rid himself of the confused idea so carefully imparted by *danseurs orientales* that the Indian dance consists mainly of snake-like movements of the hips and arms. The charm of the book should also disembarrass him of the impression given by the self-styled "critic" of Indian dancing, that it is an esoteric entertainment and hard to enjoy.

PRACTICAL INFORMATION

All Indian dancing is divided into certain categories, and those which concern only certain styles will be dealt with as the occasion arises. Here we can mention the terms *tandava* and *lasya*, which are sometimes superficially translated respectively as masculine and feminine dances; this is rather misleading. *Tandava* should imply a vigorous dance, *lasya* a soft one, and except where otherwise stated both aspects may be performed by both sexes. For instance, to illustrate the situation for Westerners, the male rôle in *Les Sylphides* might well be in the *lasya* category, with its soft and poetic flavour; whereas a brilliant technical solo for a ballerina might equally well be *tandava*. The terms refer to execution, not gender, although naturally a girl performing certain *tandava* dances such as those connected with the powerful cosmic solos of Lord Siva represents a sad infringement of taste (see *Natanam Adinar*, pp. 56–57). Also the construction of the female bosom prevents a girl from taking the *Nataraja* pose correctly (see p. 19): she should only do so in a devotional and not a representational spirit.

Mohiniattam is a dance-style which is wholly and typically *lasya*. It was prevalent in Malabar right up to the late 'twenties, and it is very largely composed of a fusion of the Tanjore temple-dance and the *Kathakali* dance style of Malabar. Tanjore and Malabar are geographically close.

The *neck-movement*—" *Rechakas* " is one word for it—is characteristic of all Indian dance-styles and consequently it tends to be exaggerated by amateurs, but it should be performed with subtlety. There are several varieties of this movement, the head gliding from side to side either slowly or quickly with the shoulders immobile. Its main functions are: *emphasis* of mood or time: *rhythmical embellishment* (as an *entrechât* in the ballet): or purely decorative. No particular virtuosity is needed to perform the neck-movement; it isn't a matter of developing extra muscles so much as discovering for oneself where the requisite muscles are situated, and controlling them accordingly.

Bare feet are a feature of Indian dancing, and here is one of the means by which the genuine Indian dancer can be recognised. *Slap-slap-slap* go his feet on the floor; he wears bells round his ankles, to be sure, but he must be able to maintain a clearly-defined rhythm without them which should be clearly audible. He often practises without bells in the same way that a ballerina practises without her blocked shoes to strengthen her feet.

The *Natya Sastra* says: "The Bells should be made of bronze or copper or silver; they should be sweet-toned, well-shaped, dainty, with asterisms for their presiding deities, tied with an indigo string, with a knot between each pair of bells. At the time of dancing there should be a hundred or two hundred for each foot, or a hundred for the right foot and two hundred for the left . . ."—the latter is probably a practical solution to the fact that most dancers will stamp harder with the right foot than with the left one. And to-day, dancers do not always tie their bells; mounted on a leather strap, or sewn to velvet-lined silk is quite common.

Investiture with bells is a great ceremony for every dancer and makes the adoption of a professional life inevitable.

Abhinaya and *bhava* cover gesture and expression. There are nine basic movements of the head, eight glances of the eye, six movements of the eyebrows, four of the neck, and at least four thousand single and combined gestures of the hands, specific postures for the body, the legs—specifications for everything, and each with its special name. But it is more practical to consider the complete study of this monumental technical curriculum as being in the province of the pundit, or scholar, and to enjoy the delights of Indian dancing with just those rudiments of technique which will increase our pleasure.

Any writer, armed with a good dictionary, can find enough complicated words to make himself seem clever. Using this method, a certain number of unprincipled persons have frightened off many good and intelligent citizens who would wish to study the elements of the Indian dance, by inferring that "the whole thing rests on understanding the gestures" and that this will involve dull, hard and difficult work. This should be contradicted at once, and unmasked as one of the methods used by the fake-critic to conserve the field of Indian-dance criticism and authority to himself. Gesture-language is a delightful art, as will be seen from the few examples on pp. 70-71, and once one gets the general idea, easy to follow. If the reader wants further information on this subject, let him procure a copy of *The Mirror of Gesture*, being original texts translated by Ananda Coomaraswamy and Duggirala Gopalakrishnayya.

As the reader will have seen, each of the classical styles comes from a different part of India, usually featuring a different physical type. Excluding society dilettantes, a dancer from one school cannot perform another style, and as a rule refuses to admit that any other important style exists. Ram Gopal, however, seems to be able to transform his mind and his body at will and to dance each style "as to the manner born". How he does so is his secret, but he is welcomed as a star-pupil by elderly and sagacious *gurus* all over India, as I have seen for myself. They know they can trust him to do them credit by showing their dances to the world in the way their tradition dictates.

INDIAN DANCING TO-DAY: THE CREATIVE DANCE: DANCE-CRITICS

In every established branch of dancing, as in politics, there is the ideal side which is little if anything short of Divine, and the practical side, which naturally falls rather short of the original ideal. Therefore to gain a true impression of the subject one is studying, both sides of the case must be constantly in one's mind.

In extolling the undeniably Divine origin of the classical dances of India, one must avoid giving the impression that every Indian dancer and teacher is a paragon of talent and a master of the ancient Hindu scriptures which relate to his particular branch of the dance, as unfortunately this is far from the truth; yet one must also remember that those scriptures and texts themselves are indeed of an incomparable excellence, vitality and wisdom, and that could the dance be performed in full accordance with them, then that dance, and its dancer, would be well beyond the powers of human description.

Ideally, not only Indian dancing but *all* dancing should be governed by certain rules, whether they are consciously or instinctively applied. That the ancient sage Bharata has these rules set down in a way which cannot be surpassed is only an accessory after this fact. In pursuit of the same ideal, one may say that whereas all Indian dancing *should* be governed by the main doctrines propounded in the *Sastras*, yet sad to relate most of the dance-masters are too fully occupied in pointing out that *their* style is the only reliable one in India to give any attention to the *Sastras*, and allowing their pupils to make exactly the same mistakes, whatever the style. This passage along the road to ruin is being vastly accelerated by the awful, sloppy style required and encouraged by the modern Indian films. (Incidentally India has a film-industry only second in size to America. There is a cinema in almost every Indian village of any size.)

With regard to creative dancing in India; as always and in any country, where creative art of any sort indicates great creative genius, it must succeed; but where it indicates that the artist has merely become "creative" because he (or she) is unable to master any of the great classical and traditional techniques, the result is poor. And that familiar type of dancer who peddles his own hotch-potch of styles in countries where he hopefully reckons he can describe himself as "classical" without discovery, is purely and simply, a fake; in India he performs Westernised dances and in the West he trades The Mysterious Orient. Even his literary admirers have now earned themselves a special nickname. They are known as "the Fakers."

Here there is a real nest of trouble for those who want to learn something of genuine Indian dancing, and most of it is caused by those self-appointed prophets who, wishing to occupy the arena of Indian dance-criticism in solitary splendour, cause a great deal of confusion by arraying many mediocre and inadequately-trained Indian dancers with the cloak of "classicism", and expressing themselves in that dull, complicated manner which, as mentioned before, terrifies the ordinary dance-lover into the belief that he will never be able to understand Indian dancing. In this book, the antics of these exasperating and meddlesome "experts" are symbolised by two fictitious personages, Sri Bhubbal of the East and Madame Zqueak, of the West. Their material equipment consists of an alarm-clock, a camera, and an airline ticket apiece (See India in Three Days!)—and their mental equipment is negligible. The word they use most and understand least is "authenticity".*

Another feature which characterises these partly-humorous, partly dangerous parasites is that they cannot or will not realise that the Indian arts are now universally recognised, that the public executions and denouncements, so to speak, have now terminated. They have a Columbus complex: they "discover" society girls who have taken up dancing, or steal little dance-apprentices from remote villages and really believe that in so doing they have made history, in the same way as E. Krishna Iyer who really did re-discover *Bharata Natya*, as will be pointed out later on, taking the trouble to learn and perform it himself, and revealing it to the Indian public through the art of the genius Balasaraswathi as late as 1934, a time when a crusade really was necessary if Indian art and dancing was to survive at all. Here we may content ourselves with a quotation from E. B. Havell's *Himalayas in Indian Art:*—"Decadent or mediocre art should be recognised as such, whether it be Eastern or Western. It cannot be raised to a higher plane by copious libations of exuberant verbiage . . . though that may be less harmful than the former indifference and condemnation."

The reader may wonder why I make continual references to the less attractive side of Indian dancing with its misunderstandings, prejudices and knaveries. Why not stick to the delightful movements, costumes and so forth? The answer is that recently, the delightful costumes and movements were in real danger of effecting a complete disappearance, and without examining the reasons for this near-calamity, the picture of Indian dancing would remain incomplete. The Indian dance has survived the bombastic attacks of the "Anti-Nautch Party" of the 'twenties, which forbade and denounced all forms of dancing as disgusting and immoral; it now has to survive the attentions of dilettantes, Bhubbal-and-Zqueaks, etc., and the object of this book is to give the reader a basic knowledge of the genuine dances of India which will make him independent of spurious criticism and fake-performers, thus helping to save the Indian dance from what might well prove to be its final disappearance as a great and vital art-form.

At present the chief danger is that of over-popularity, in which the real dance can disappear as completely as it did when Pavlova was seeking it in 1929, when it was completely obscured by decadence and social prejudice.

The dance that has fascinated the ballet throughout its development is that of the *bayadères*—in other words, ancient *Bharata Natya*, and the idea of the vestal virgin who dedicates her life to the service of a temple-god is one of enduring fascination. If only Pavlova had thought of searching in out-of-the-way temples, and witnessed some of the performances of the real *bayadères* or *devadasis*, what might not have happened! And if only Nijinsky, struggling against the more

* See the back endpapers.

conventional dictates of classical ballet and fascinated by the legends of the Blue God (Sri Krishna) had met Kunju Kurup, in Malabar, or Meenakshi Sundaram Pillai, hidden in Tanjore, what might not have been accomplished!

But the first and so far the only person to introduce the names of such masters to the West, and to a great extent to the East as well, has been Ram Gopal. He has told us the names of the masters and shown us their styles. If it were not for him, the world at large would still be entirely ignorant of these Vestrises and Cecchettis of the Indian Dance, who would pass away taking their secrets with them, as too many have done in the past.

BOOKS ON INDIAN SUBJECTS: A SHORT-CUT TO UNDERSTANDING

If this book should inflame the reader with a desire to study classical Indian literature, art, and so forth, he will have an interesting time, but if he thinks he is going to study as we study history in the West, in a chronological and organised form, he is in for a shock. The available literature in English on Indian subjects, with certain exceptions, is divided into three distinct categories: first, books written by professors for the benefit of other professors, who write a thesis on, for example, the *Rig Veda*, and plough solemnly on without telling you what the *Rig Veda* is, assuming that you already know; secondly, a less respectable collection of books written by ignoramuses who supply you with opinions instead of facts. So there you are, with one set of books in which elemental facts are omitted because the author assumes you will be aware of them, and another set in which facts are omitted because the author is ignorant of them himself.

The third category is heartening and, of course, the smallest of the three, and contains books written by those who are masters of their subject and can therefore afford to write simply and understandably. As mentioned earlier, a list of such books has been added to this volume.

THE TECHNICAL SKETCHES

These are to help the Indian dancer to understand and perform authentic dance-styles and to help the dance-lover to recognise them. But the dancer should beware of trying to give a serious performance in any one of these dances without having proper training with a genuine and authentic dance-teacher, such as those named in this book, or their real disciples. The drawings are all made under such instruction, but nothing can replace a real *guru*, or master.

The dance-lover in the West who has not yet seen real Indian dancing will naturally get much more out of this book when the opportunity comes.

The sequences of dance-sketches have sometimes been drawn moving to the left first instead of to the right, which is more usual; this is because it is easier to follow a sequence starting from the left side of a page than otherwise.

Difficult names and terms have been listed for reference in an appendix at the end of the book. Most of the districts and places mentioned herein are indicated in a map which will be found on the front endpapers.

CHAPTER I

GODS AND MYTHOLOGY IN INDIAN DANCING

INTRODUCTION

The term "Indian Gods" can convey very different images to the average mind. The old *idées fixes* of the Western world in general concerning Hindu gods, and their association with outlandishness, paganism, frightful sacrifices and "rude sculptures" has been more or less buried for ever. The devout Catholic kneeling before his picture of the gentle Madonna has learned to respect the devout Hindu prostrating himself before kindly Vishnu the preserver, or some other deity, and the Hindu philosopher readily accepts the beauty of Christianity based as it is on Divine love. The past, with its frightful sacrifices in the East, has been successfully balanced up against the inquisitions and persecution of the West, and duly cancelled out. Indians may embrace Christianity if they please; in general humble worshippers may now glorify the Supreme Being in the manner they wish, the merits of mutual toleration have been discovered and proved, and the artist may rejoice.

But the Westerner, although his general attitude has changed from one of righteous, non-comprehending indignation and passed *via* patronising tolerance to a deep respect for Indian art and all that goes with it, still finds himself in a tangle when it comes to reaching an understanding of, for example, beings with four or more arms, beings who are half snakes, beings with inscrutable faces and crossed legs, and the like. This is only natural, as such beings are outside his orbit of experience, having taken thousands of years to reach their present position and status in the Hindu Pantheon, and having been developed in accordance with the needs and racial traditions of hundreds of millions of people whose surroundings, life, food and physique are entirely different to those of the Western peoples, who suffer a poverty and illiteracy to a degree unknown elsewhere, yet who witness marvels of Nature and mankind's magnificence on a scale undreamed of outside vast India.

The fabulous beauty, power and grace of figures in Indian sculpture in which the very stone seems to be illuminated from within by the humble fervour of the unknown and consummate sculptors seem to have received their first widespread recognition as a great art-form from the French, a vivacious, quick, intelligent and art-loving race whose ready acceptance of sex as a reality which may be discussed without embarrassment when the occasion arises has enabled them to appreciate Indian art in its entirety without the prejudices and reserve which characterise the more stolid Anglo-Saxon. French books on Indian art, from the point of view of pure information, are amongst the finest. But once the Anglo-Saxon discovers an art and succeeds in finding an echo in it for his own spirit, that art has a staunch supporter who will be unmoved by the vagaries of

PLATE I

Above and on left : Ram Gopal dances in the historic temple of Belur, Mysore
State. *Right :* Ram Gopal stands in front of the giant Jain statue of Buddha,
Mysore.

PLATE II

Top Left: Conjeevaram (Kanchipuram).　*Right:*
Mambara Palace of Lights, Lucknow.

Centre Left: Bhuvaneshwar: Raja Rani.　*Right:*
Channakesava Temple, Belur, Mysore.

Bottom Left: Konarak, the Black Pagoda.　*Right:*
Mysore, illumination of palace.

Photographs by courtesy of H.E. the High Commissioner for India.

fashionable thought. To-day, through the art of Ram Gopal, the Indian dance has conquered that most difficult and conservative of all audiences, the British public, who with their wits sharpened by war and suffering have suddenly understood the perpetual wars and sufferings of India, and allowed themselves to be soothed by the ancient dances of India in the same way that India has soothed herself for countless thousands of years. Children are clamouring to learn the various movements and ballet-dancers yearn for Indian suppleness and self-possession. Countries of Europe and America, flocking to the Indian dance, feel instinctively that their own dances are an echo of this ancient art. They read books on Indian subjects, ask questions of any Indian, and the more muddled the information, the more determined they become to get the essential facts sorted out. So here is some advice.

Legends of India should be read whilst bearing in mind that *Indian gods and goddesses are idealised men and women.* They are not identified with the Supreme Being, but each deity is an aspect of the One. They have human qualities; they are sometimes jealous and vindictive, often petty and are not above telling a few lies when in a tight mythological corner; but the myths are always allegorical and as a whole may be understood to show humans how the gods and goddesses achieved Divine perfection—which in turn is symbolised by physical perfection in marvellous sculptures and bronzes. Supernatural powers are symbolised by a superhuman number of arms, for example. Sagacity and earthly wisdom are embodied in the elephant-headed god, Ganesha or Ganapathi, the scribe of the *Mahabharata* and the pet of the other gods, who rides on a rat which is known in India for its resourcefulness. The legend of how Ganesha got his head is delightful, but there is no room for it here. But it will be understood how the Indian gods, monstrous, intimidating or obscure as they may seem at first sight, gradually form characters as one studies them, so that in the end it is not difficult to see how they fulfil their function in the Indian home—one might almost say they are treated as a member of the family who is entitled to great veneration. They are "for those who need them". The sage meditates alone; he doesn't need a tangible reminder of the Infinite Wisdom, and partly on this account he is deeply respected. The real yogi is also an object of great regard, but there are fake yogis, just as there are fake dancers. The alleged

SRI RAMA
—THE HERO OF THE "RĀMAYĀNA."
(South Indian bronze, 14ᵗʰ century.)

resemblance of yogism to great dancing isn't nearly as complicated as is often suggested. Briefly, the dancer controls his muscles with the object of performing physical feats beyond the scope of the ordinary man, whilst the yogi controls *his* muscles with a Divine object, that of gaining complete control of his mind for a spiritual purpose.

The idea that Indian dancing is solely religious is substantially correct, but it has given rise to some rather strange conjectures. People who have felt or sensed the tremendous hidden power of the devotional dance ask if it is not wrong to perform such dances on the stage, and whether they should not be confined to temples? To which one may reply that there are some dances which no one is ever likely to see, and some of these are alluded to later on. But in India, as in the West, there is no general attempt to confine all religious works to places of worship alone. In the West, few people have any objection to a painting of the Madonna being displayed in a picture-gallery, or in someone's home: but naturally everyone agrees that such works must on no account be put to base uses. With this reservation in mind, then, we may safely affirm that in many aspects the Indian devotional dance may be performed, seen and admired in any building, provided that it is presented with dignity and restraint.

The intricate legends, the staggering array of gods and their various incarnations can be studied in a number of excellent literary works, some of which are listed at the end of this book. The purpose of this short essay is simply to acquaint the reader with the attitude of mind in which he will most easily assimilate this fantastically complicated matter, in order to associate its essential characteristics with the living and vital classical Indian dance—in which the very essence of these supernatural beings should appear before us, even as it distinguishes the wonderful sculptures and bronzes.

On the next few pages is a collection of sketches showing some of the principal deities of the Hindu Pantheon, and those who are most likely to be seen represented in some way in the Indian dance. In conclusion, for the benefit of the reader to whom the question of Indian gods and mythology is quite foreign, here are a few basic facts from the framework of Indian history, which is inextricably involved with mythology, that will help him to sort things out.

The *Vedic period* (about 1500–800 B.C.) is so-called because the four Vedas were composed during that time. They are respectively the Rig Veda, the oldest; Yajurveda; Samaveda, and Atharvaveda. They are largely accounts of invading Aryan tribes who entered India about 1500 B.C. and besides their mythological content supply information that a far older culture than the one the Aryans brought with them already existed in India at that time. Each Veda consists of two parts; hymns, and ritualistic precepts. The *Upanishads* are attached to the latter and contain mystical doctrine.

The 18 *Puranas*, the Vishnu Purana being the most comprehensive, which speak mainly of the mythical and legendary activities of the Celestials; the *Mahabharata* (sometimes known as the "fifth Veda") which contains the famous battle between the honest Pandavas and the sneering Kurus, symbolising the triumph of Good over Evil; and the *Ramayana*, an epic concerning the famous legends of Rama and Sita, form the main bulk of Hindu sacred literature.

A SMALL DRUM, OR "DAMARU" SYMBOLISING RHYTHM OF CREATION.

GANGA, RIVER-GODDESS

(HAIR)

CASSIA LEAVES

FIRE, SYMBOLISING DESTRUCTION

MOON

SERPENT

HANDS:
"FEAR NOT,"
"FOR I AM HERE"

"MY FOOT HELD ALOFT GIVES RELEASE"

TIGER-SKIN

THE MALEVOLENT DWARF, "TRIPURA" (OR MUYALAKHA, ETC.) SYMBOLICAL OF EVIL OVERCOME.

"TORANA" OR ARCH OF FLAMES

LOTUS-PEDESTAL

RINGS FOR TRANS-PORTING IMAGE DURING FESTIVALS ETC.

ŚIVA AS NATARAJA:
(OR, LORD OF THE DANCE,)
SOUTH INDIA: MIXED METALS.

—From an image of great antiquity: Ram Gopal Collection.

BELOW: AN UNUSUAL VERSION OF ŚIVA'S DANCE. (South Indian Bronze.)

(Don't confuse with KRISHNA on KALIYA, on following page.)

BELOW: ŚIVA AS A MENDICANT, OR YOGI IN MEDITATION. (From an original North Indian painting, 18th century. Ram Gopal collection.)

ŚIVA, LORD OF THE DANCE

These two pages show Lord Siva, or Mahadeva (Great God), in just a few of the forms in which he is to be seen represented in Indian art. Almost every Hindu deity has two different aspects, the god or superman and a very human being, and sometimes he is very difficult to identify. "So-and-so walked with Agni", says a myth. Does it mean Agni the god of fire, or does it mean that the person held a lighted torch? It is better not to be too pedantic, for it is easy to enjoy the stories and pictures as they come, and after a little, understanding follows.

ŚIVA dancing
"SANDHYA
NRTTA MURTI"-
His Dance of the
Setting Sun:
(Copper.
CEYLON,
10ᵗʰ -13ᵗʰ
century.)

B

Right: (A)
RAM GOPAL as ŚIVA in his
"Dance of the Setting Sun."
Pose showing that "the
hair of the Lord swayed
as He danced....."
(See sketch B. above
for completed
movement.)

A.

Siva as a god represents Creation, Preservation, and Destruction. These three processes are regarded as a cycle and are symbolised by a mythological dance. The most famous specimen of the Nataraja is the one from the great Śiva Temple in Tanjore, the figure alone being nearly four feet high and of an incomparable grace, dignity and beauty.

As for Śiva's character as he is known and loved in India; he is hot-tempered, susceptible to female charm, adores jewellery, loves smashing things and then celebrating with one of his wild dances. He is also shown distracted by grief at the death of his wife, after which he remains a tormented wanderer, only being comforted when a further incarnation of his wife comes to him on Mount Kailasa. Or he is a *rishi*, silent and imperturbable on that sacred mountain; a yogi, or a beggar, living from a bowl which has become one of his symbols.

His *Dance of the Setting Sun* balances all his qualities. It is sometimes performed in a spirit of deep devotion, in the full glow of the sunset on a mountain top, by all manner of persons, ranging from wealthy maharajas to penniless sages. To have seen Ram Gopal's fine interpretation of this ancient dance, is to have seen the essence of Siva.

KRISHNA, THE BLUE GOD

Krishna is the eighth *avatar* (incarnation) of Vishnu; he was sent to the human world on this occasion to rescue it from the demon Kansa. (Vishnu is to have one more incarnation, and with the world as it is to-day, it seems to be about time he came.) As Krishna, he has his own life-story, and also figures in other epics, for example as the warrior Arjuna's charioteer in the famous *Mahabharata* battle. On this occasion he delivered the whole *Bhagavad Gita* to Arjuna, whose spirits were flagging at the thought of killing his own relatives and friends. The *Bhagavad Gita* is known to Westerners by the translation of Sir Edwin Arnold's *Song Celestial*. It is as dear to Hindus as the Psalms are to Christians.

KRISHNA: DANCE-POSE BY RAM GOPAL.

BALA-KRISHNA (WITH STOLEN BUTTER-BALLS:) small brass figure, South India

SYMBOLS OF KRISHNA: (South Indian bronze)

FLUTE   CHAKRA   CONCH-SHELL

KRISHNA AS THE CHILD-HERO DANCING ON THE SERPENT KALIYA. (South Indian Bronze.)

Krishna in his lifetime became a distinguished ruler, diplomat and soldier. But the Krishna who is loved by millions of Hindus is when he is in his role as a mischievous, resourceful baby, then as a youth who tended cows and played with other cowherds in Vrindavan. With his yellow *dhoti*, blue skin and his black eyes sparkling with fun, he got up to every prank a fertile mind could devise, pinching butter and milk, teasing the life out of the milkmaids or *gopis*—but he could extract himself from the militant consequences of any scrape with the aid of the celestial music he could conjure from his flute. He is wholly lovable, thoroughly spankable, but every tale of him has an allegorical meaning.

KRISHNA   RADHA

CYMBALS:

MRDANG

TAMBURA

RAS LEELA

"Hearing the love-call of Krishna's flute, the *gopis* left their husbands and went in search of him. When the ladies came the lord of their hearts said, "I just wanted you to see the beauty of this moonlit night. Now you can go back to your husbands". Heart-broken, the *gopis* cried out "But we have left our husbands and children because you woke us, and now you leave us in mid air! How can you treat us so cruelly?"

"Then Krishna smiled and multiplied himself, danced with each one of the *gopis*, and every lady thought he loved her best."

But Krishna's favourite was Radha, Ayanogosha's wife, and although reasonably enough the latter felt jealous at first, in the end he became one of Lord Krishna's greatest devotees. The allegory concerns the response of the human soul to the call of the Divine. (The *Ras Leela* ballet is popular to-day, when it may contain any one of Krishna's classical pranks with the *gopis*.)

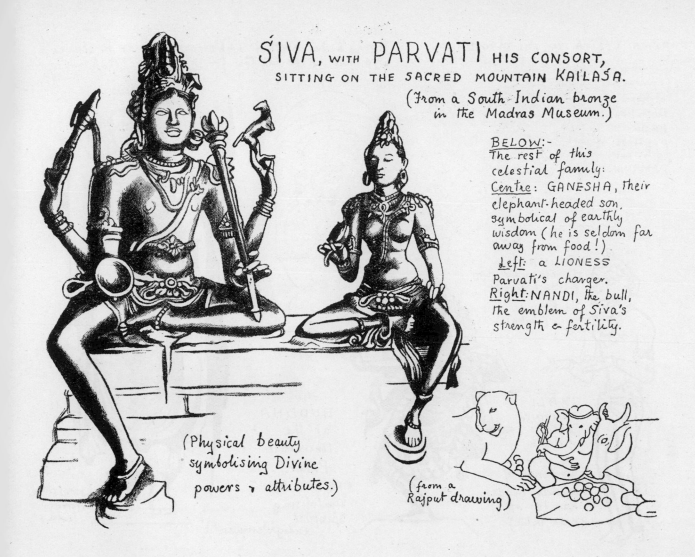

SIVA, WITH PARVATI HIS CONSORT,
SITTING ON THE SACRED MOUNTAIN KAILASA.
(From a South Indian bronze
in the Madras Museum.)

BELOW:-
The rest of this
celestial family:
Centre: GANESHA, their
elephant-headed son,
symbolical of earthly
wisdom (he is seldom far
away from food!).
Left: a LIONESS
Parvati's charger.
Right: NANDI, the bull,
the emblem of Siva's
strength & fertility.

(Physical beauty
symbolising Divine
powers & attributes.)

(from a
Rajput drawing)

INDIAN IDEALS OF PHYSICAL BEAUTY

Behold all-powerful Siva and his gentle consort Parvati sitting on sacred
Mount Kailasa. They can be given a hundred and one interpretations, some
celestial and some in relation to more material considerations, such as idealised
matrimonial harmony. They are gracing this page because of their superb proportions and appearance, as a fair example of the Indian ideals of physical beauty.

Before enquiring into the separate stipulations governing these ideals, one
thing at least must be made abundantly clear, and this is that the master-artist
who fashioned these two majestic figures was certainly more concerned with
what their beauty represented than with the creation of beauty in itself. It is
obvious that the artist was a master of his medium, and it should be noted that
he used his skill to express a spiritual ideal, not simply to create two beautiful
figures; hence the unmistakable air of godliness evinced by those two personages.
They are real deities—in other words, at first sight we are more strongly aware
of their celestial import than of their actual proportions. The artist, having
achieved complete mastery of his tools and technique, was free and able to express

RAMA & SITA IN THE MAGIC CAR, "PUSHPAKA."

(Drawings of Rama, etc. taken from Hindu paintings of the epic, "RAMAYANA")

RAMA & his brother LAKSHMAN dress in leaves & go into exile in the forest. with SITA, Rama's wife.

HANUMAN, The MONKEY-GOD, faithful friend to Rama. (Ceylon)

KĀLI DANCING. Goddess of death, she wears garlands of human heads, hands, etc.. (North India.)

THE BUDDHA as the Universal Pillar. (Physical beauty symbolising spiritual enlightenment.)

(Sandstone, North India.)

in inanimate metal transcendental qualities which have nothing to do with mere anatomy and craftsmanship; in just the way that a dancer who has absolute mastery over a great technique should be able to evoke spiritual subtleties which have nothing to do with the muscular control of his arms and legs.

Therefore it will be understood that all Indian art is judged by its spiritual implications in the belief that beauty belongs to the human mind. Technical capability is disregarded unless used to express an ideal. It is in this respect that Indian ideals differ so entirely from those of the West as they are to-day.

Thus to classify the various requisites of Indian physical beauty without first insisting on its Divine implications would be as useless as making a catalogue of the colours in a sunset, with the belief that in so doing one has created a masterpiece.

The ideal male figure is generally described with the aid of various similes. His body, it is said, should taper to a waist like the leaf of a peepul-tree; he should be as supple as the stem of a lotus-bud. There is a great insistence that the figure of a man should resemble that of a lion. The superman is described in the

Mahabharata as a type of mighty hunter who in desperate conflict with the King of Beasts, has become invincible and acquired a lion-like body, a broad chest and shoulders, a sturdy neck and a very slim waist; long arms and legs being indicative of nobility. (It is to be noticed that the Minoan dandies of 3000 B.C. used tight lacing to appear slim-waisted, and that to-day highly ferocious hill-tribes on the borders of Tibet pull in their waists till they look like figures-of-eight.)

The exquisite torsoes of the sculptured Bhuddas, with their soft rounded shoulders and silken skins, are a less warlike interpretation of physical beauty as encasing and symbolising an enlightened mind. The physical ideals of Indian beauty are nowhere represented with such freedom and mastery as in the miraculous paintings which people the walls of the famous Ajanta Caves. The figure of Śiva seems to be a fusion of the best qualities of the various ideals of Indian masculine beauty.

Concerning female ideals of beauty; after examining the proportions and bearing of Parvati, and the other sketches from classical paintings, sculptures, etc., of beautiful Indian girls and women, there is no need to go any further. But the following "disqualifications of a *danseuse*" from the ancient texts are worth quoting: "The ten kinds of women unacceptable in drama are those whose eyes are speckled, whose hair is scanty, whose lips are thick, or breasts pendant, who are very stout or very thin, or very tall or very short, who are hump-backed, or have not a good voice."

"Vulgar dancing" is described as that which does not begin with an invocation, etc., and awful calamities are predicted to fall upon those who witness such a dance. The treatise proceeds: "What is said traditionally by our ancestors must be kept in view. Having made the invocation, etc., the dancing may begin. The song should be sustained in the throat; the mood (*bhava*) must be shown by the glances; time (*tala*) is marked by the feet. For wherever the hand moves, there the glances follow; where the glances go, the mind follows; where the mind goes, the mood follows; where the mood goes, there is the flavour (*rasa*)."

CHAPTER II

INDIAN MUSIC

In choosing which instruments to sketch on pages 28 and 29 I had to exercise iron self-discipline. Indian musical instruments are food for the painter and the poet as well as for the musically-minded, and the varieties of each kind, of which there is an enormous number, run into dozens. How delightful to sketch that variety of veena which has two gourd-resonators connected by a hollow tube, which the ladies play over their shoulders in the miniature paintings! —but you, dear reader, are more likely to encounter the model I have sketched, and there isn't room for the other.

Musically, India and the West meet in some folk-dance tunes (people who sow corn and harvest the results naturally make the same movements and to the same rhythms all the world over). They meet in certain conventional rhythms for the drums; and they meet in certain respects over the flute. The Western Nature-god, Pan, as he plays his mythological pipes by the river at evening and dawn, awakes echoes in our deepest souls which recall the flute of Krishna, the legendary Blue God who lives on to-day in the magic of the Indian flutist, whether "natural" or sophisticated. The latter plays a concert-flute and has often tremendous technical mastery of his instrument in addition to a pleasing tone; and the simpler, shepherd's flute has a surpassing sweetness and sadness, a nostalgia evocative of the lush, dewy pastures of India, which can be appreciated by any and every one who hears it. A fine flutist, in India, can command the wildest salary and behave however he wishes, and anyone who has heard the unearthly beauty of the Indian flute as it drops notes one by one, like jewels, into the silent glory of the Indian dusk, will sympathise with me in my struggle to describe the indescribable; that magical melody which can take a girl from her lover or unite the soul with the Infinite.

The notes of the flute, then, will serve as a bridge across the gap between the music of the East and the West; and even if we cannot quite cross from one side to the other, at least we may stand in the middle and see elemental Pan piping away in the reeds one side, and Krishna standing with crossed feet and his flute aslant, playing his celestial notes amongst the lotus-flowers on the other.

Most of the difficulties of the Westerner when he tries to listen intelligently to Indian music arise over the melodic side and by now he is pretty used to being told that in the West, much delicacy of hearing has been lost; and whilst admitting that this is very true, and that it is largely due to our Western method of notation in which subtleties have been lost as they cannot be indicated in musical scripts, which is also the reason for the lost art of improvisation which cannot be used in an orchestra; and also admitting that to an Indian listener the pianoforte, with its limited intervals, may well sound like an instrument of percussion; yet it is only fair to draw the reader's attention to the fact that in India itself the highly specialised Carnatic music of the South bores Northerners to extinction, whereas the classical songs of the North are not understood at all in the South.

There is a great deal of misunderstanding between Indian and Western musicians and most of it is due to each one taking the other's music at its surface value. In India, the same considerations apply to music as those which apply to art—technique is necessary but only secondary in importance to artistic expression. Therefore in India anyone who can play an instrument with expression is accounted a musician. In the West, the same thing does not apply. Then there is the question of *raga* or *rag*, generally translated rather superficially as "melody". A *raga* is a given scale (all the classical *ragas* having different names and uses) using certain notes and leaving out others—perhaps with one set for climbing the scale and another for descending—on which the real melody is based. Therefore the melody itself, as we understand the term, is often extemporary, but based on and limited by the scale indicated by the chosen *raga*. The key is referred to as *sruti*.

The usual function of melody in Indian dancing is in many respects quite unlike that of Western accompaniment. The latter provides mood, and a basic time for the dancer. But in Indian dancing, particularly in the *Kathak* style and also in *Bharata Natya*, the melody is used to inform the audience and dancer of the number of beats to be danced as recurrent groups; and the spectator can hear when the dancer has made a mistake rather than see it, by his failure to finish on the beat *sum*, as described later.

The emphasis of that beat *sum* is the reason for the apparent competition between an Indian instrumentalist and drummer (in the West when such a recital takes place, we can see that great fun and excitement is going on but can't fathom what it is all about). The drummer has to guess just which groups of beats will be chosen by the instrumentalist for the punctuations of *sum;* and there they sit nodding away and watching each other, and great applause and appreciation is won from an Indian audience when the two musicians reach a simultaneous climax.

The highly-specialised art of giving the verbal, almost onomatopœic accompaniment to dancers such as those of *Bharata Natya*, *Kathak* and *Manipuri* makes Westerners ask "Is it a song, or is the man telling the dancer what to do?" It is a cross between the two, and in *Bharata Natya* the *natuvan* who gives the words also marks the movements of the dance with a pair of tiny gold cymbals called *talam*. His presence is so necessary to the dancer that he is in a position to practise a little tyranny, and his services are bargained for like a first-class footballer in the West. Some of the simplest of these word-sequences are marked at the foot of technical dance-sketches, as will be seen later on; they are called *bols*, which Ram Gopal descriptively translates as "winged words".

In conclusion here is a description from *Pradosha Stotra* of the orchestra of Lord Siva, as he prepares to dance: "Saraswathi plays on the veena, Indra on the flute, Brahma plays the time-marking cymbals, Lakshmi begins a song, Vishnu plays on a drum, and all the gods stand round about. . . ."—The music of the spheres, surely.

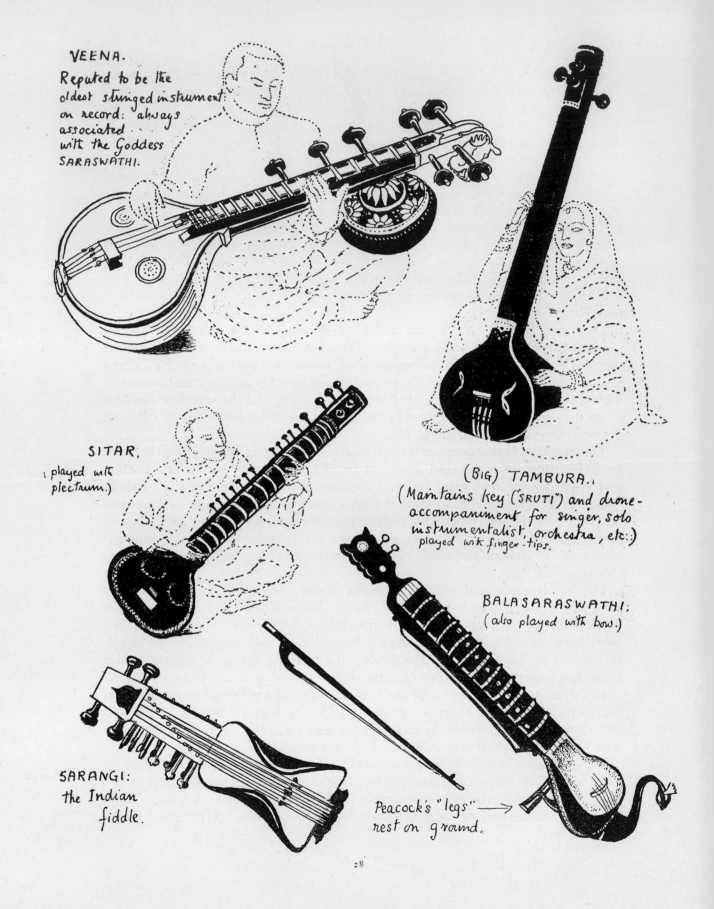

VEENA.
Reputed to be the oldest stringed instrument on record: always associated with the Goddess SARASWATHI.

SITAR,
(played with plectrum.)

(BIG) TAMBURA..
(Maintains key ("SRUTI") and drone-accompaniment for singer, solo instrumentalist, orchestra, etc:) played with finger-tips.

BALASARASWATHI:
(also played with bow.)

SARANGI:
the Indian fiddle.

Peacock's "legs" →
rest on ground.

28

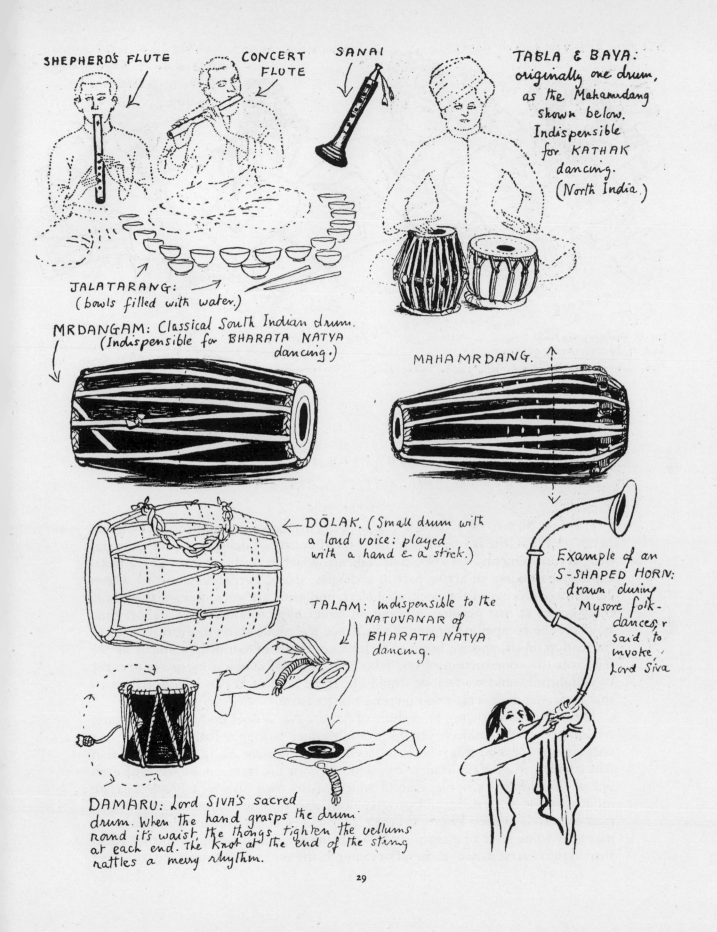

SHEPHERD'S FLUTE   CONCERT FLUTE   SANAI

TABLA & BAYA: originally one drum, as the Mahamrdang shown below. Indispensible for KATHAK dancing. (North India.)

JALATARANG: (bowls filled with water.)

MRDANGAM: Classical South Indian drum. (Indispensible for BHARATA NATYA dancing.)

MAHAMRDANG.

DOLAK. (Small drum with a loud voice: played with a hand & a stick.)

TALAM: indispensible to the NATUVANAR of BHARATA NATYA dancing.

Example of an S-SHAPED HORN: drawn during Mysore folk-dances, r said to invoke Lord Siva

DAMARU: Lord SIVA'S sacred drum. When the hand grasps the drum round it's waist, the thongs tighten the vellums at each end. The knot at the end of the string rattles a merry rhythm.

29

CELESTIAL BHARATA NATYA DANCERS:
*CHOLA-PERIOD MURALS, concealed in dark passages under huge *vimana**
of Brihadeshwaram Temple, Tanjore.

DANSEUSE:
(N.B.:
These mural-paintings had to be sketched by lamplight. How were they painted with such success —?)

MALE DANCER. (SHOWERING LOTUS PETALS) (FROM THE CLOUDS.)

MUSICIANS:

*CHOLA PERIOD= circa. 9ᵗʰ – 13ᵗʰ centuries A.D.
*VIMANA= main tower-like structure.

CHAPTER III

BHARATA NATYA

INTRODUCTION

The first impact of a *Bharata Natya* performance on an audience which has never seen it before is one of surprise at the diversity of delicate and rather extraordinary movements. To a Western audience which is unaccustomed to see facial expressions taking an active part in a classical dance curriculum, and to whom certain movements of the neck, shoulders, and arms are very strange, the whole thing seems at first peculiar, and indeed rather monotonous. After a short time however the compelling power of this dance technique starts to exert its ancient fascination on us, and we begin to feel the same sort of curiosity about it as we feel over the construction of our favourite pieces of classical music. It disturbs us delightfully, and we feel we would like some kind of key to open the door to that understanding which will increase our pleasure.

Although the following brief study of *Bharata Natya* does no more than scratch the surface of the subject, yet the whole chapter is longer than any other one chapter in this book: this is because I have chosen *Bharata Natya*, of all the Indian dance styles, to give the reader some indication of the tremendous scope of each one of the different schools; each of which has its own history, its own separate influences, social, artistic, and geographical; and although there is not room to treat each style at such length, yet the reader will be able to see for himself that to master any one style of classical Indian dancing, one must go much further afield than to the nearest dance-teacher. For example, the ancient sculptures and paintings are a far safer guide to correct costume than the muddled and gaudy confections often worn on the Indian dance-stage to-day.

For the purpose of the survey of *Bharata Natya* we must investigate the subject from three different angles: (*a*) its beginning, which is shrouded in the remotest antiquity; (*b*) its recent and complete disappearance from respectable life in India; (*c*) its present-day renaissance and those responsible; and finally, an account of the contemporary programme of this ancient dance as accepted to-day by the modern savants and intelligent dance-public. This section is concluded with technical notes and sketches giving just a taste of *Bharata Natya* as it should, and should not be seen at the present time.

A GENERAL SURVEY: PAST TILL PRESENT

Bharata's *Natya Sastras** is a monumental work which deals amongst other things with the arts of drama and the dance and which, according to ancient Indian mythology, was compiled at the request of the gods, conceived by Brahma, and written by the sage Bharata during a period of Divine inspiration. The palm-leaves inscribed with ancient Sanskrit text are preserved to this day in the great temple libraries of Tanjore and Malabar, and are frequently studied by the wise Sanskrit pundits in their researches in music, drama, dance, medicine and literature. It is rather ironical to note that with a very few exceptions, all the present day *Bharata Natya* "nattuvans" (singers and instructors for the dance) in South India are completely ignorant of the Sanskrit texts and their contents, and are playing no little part in confusing artistic values in the new rebirth of this rare dance form.

It should be born in mind that the *Bharata Natya Sastras*, whilst governing the whole of the application of the classic dances of India, should not be confused with *Bharata Natya*, which last is the term used to describe the ancient secular dance of the Tanjore *bayadères*. Incidentally, the name *Bharata* is said to be composed of the first syllables of the following words:—

BHAva (or inner spiritual feeling expressed outwardly or visibly),

RAga (or melody), and

TAla (or rhythm).

As to the age of the *Sastras*, this can only be conjectured; but the great antiquity of the work is undeniable for its actual conception is buried in mythological times, when gods still walked amongst humans on the earth, and men had not yet lost the power to see them.

For thousands of years therefore Indian gods have been worshipped through the medium of fantastic and beautiful dances, which naturally made a strong appeal to the great contemporary sculptors throughout the passing ages, and they froze the swirling, leaping and undulating figures into a matchless record of rhythmic grace. And just as those unknown but consummate sculptors were inspired by the vital skill and supple beauty of the nameless dancers of their day, so must the serious Indian dance student seek to recapture that inspiration, and try to revitalise his art by studying the sculptures until his own movements become impregnated by those matchless records of dancing, where time has, for once, stood still, for the benefit of the contemporary dancer. In much the same spirit the contemporary

* Bharata's *Science of Dancing*.

ballet-student in the West tries to enrich his art by studying the old lithographs of Taglioni and Vestris, and the photographs of Nijinsky and Pavlova which remain to us to-day.

THE DEGRADATION AND DISAPPEARANCE OF *BHARATA NATYA*

Despite the great esteem in which this elegant, refined and highly religious dance was held, it is not hard to understand how it gradually tended towards degradation, propounding as it did such a subject as Divine love, and danced by such dancers! Eventually, rich Indian noblemen started to employ these *devadasis* (literally "Servants of God", also called *bayadères*) in their palaces. With their innate love of the rare and the beautiful, the princes soon saw that these wonderfully-trained and lovely girls would provide a surpassingly piquant entertainment in their courts. They gave large sums to the girls and their teachers, with the result that the dances soon came to be addressed, not to a deity, but to the maharajah or prince in question; with the dance-teachers all competing with one another as to who could produce the most erotic dances and the most seductive pupils as bait for untold wealth and patronage.

These marvellous girl-dancers could demand very high salaries and their services were expensive. They travelled long distances and were often retained at courts very far from their South Indian homes; as an example one may take Gauribai of Baroda who was employed for over fifty years by the late Maharajah of Baroda. But she was "imported" from Tanjore. The sketch of the girl on p. 37 shows the costume for a *devadasi* as was generally seen at that time; the "apron" front, the satin pyjamas, are alien influences; the lines of the figure, which the dance displays to perfection, are almost completely obliterated; a silhouette which women taking to this dance-art to-day would do well to avoid, if they would look like dancers and not bundles of unwashed laundry, animated by head, arms and legs! The sketch of the figure of *Dipa-Lakshmi* on the same page shows a version of the classical silhouette, forming the basis of Ram Gopal's own costume design for *Bharata Natya*—which is shown on p. 42, and which, with a little adjustment for the present demands of society, retains the flavour of the original sculptures and reveals the movements of the dancer, instead of the heavy, overdressed and *demodé* appearance of that other Victorianised horror.

The dance remained an art, despite royal whims and extravagances (*Bharata Natya* being "too remote a goddess" to be easily learned), until it became the custom for girls and women to perform lewd and suggestive dances at village weddings, to entertain foreigners, and so on; this custom earned an evil reputation for the "nautch-dance", and resulted in the complete degradation and disrepute for *Bharata Natya*, and indeed ultimately for practically the whole of the classical dances of India, as far as society was concerned; and except in very few cases the *devadasi* system, which had for thousands of years preserved the ancient dance in its true form, became decadent and misunderstood. Foreigners thought they saw a connection between the erotic sculptures with which some temples are decorated and this version of the nautch-dance, and they wrote indignant and condemnatory articles on the subject which described *all* Indian dancing as abominable; and this seems to have given many Western-educated Indians a

PLATE III

Above, left to right: The late Ponniah Pillai, Ram Gopal, and Meenakshi Sundaram Pillai.

It is in the house of Ponniah Pillai and his ancestors, in West Street, Tanjore, that the purest and greatest traditions of South Indian Carnatic music, dancing and drama have been preserved and taught, right up to the present day. It is from this house that Meenakshi Sundaram Pillai acquired his art of *Bharata Natya*, under the instruction of traditional " natuvanars." Ram Gopal has been working at the remorseless *Bharata Natya* technique to such an extent that in this photograph tired lines under his eyes are clearly noticeable.

Left : Ram Gopal with M. S. Pillai, on his recent visit to India.

PLATE IV

Ram Gopal in two poses from a *Bharata Natya* " Padam "—an item in which a poem, sung by the musicians, must be interpreted by the dancer, who must use all the story-teller's art in addition to a perfect dance-technique.   An expressive face is an absolute necessity.

SCULPTURES TAKEN FROM CHIDAM-
BARAM TEMPLE, SOUTH INDIA, PART
OF WHICH DATES FROM BEFORE 6TH
CENT: A.D.: FIGURES CARVED CIRCA
12TH CENT., & REPRESENT CONTEM-
PORARY DANCE INTERPRETATION OF
NATYA SASTRA TEXTS, "108 KARANAS"
BEING SHOWN IN AS MANY FIGURES.
ON RIGHT: THE SCULPTORS, AS SEEN
BY THEMSELVES. COMPLETE WITH
MEASURING-ROD, SAID TO HAVE
BEEN A UNIT OF 8½ FEET, DIVIDED
INTO 6 PARTITIONS AS SHOWN.

mistaken inferiority-complex regarding their dances and arts, from which they are only just recovering.

The result was that from the middle of the 19th century to the first quarter of the 20th, dancing in India went into almost complete oblivion. At this time the "Anti-Nautch Campaign", as it was known, was in full blast. (In all art history, Grundyism in the ascendant has always marked Philistinism rampant, and art in decline; in this case, a fair example is provided by a Miss Tenant, who made the journey all the way from England to India to pursuade cultured Indians to boycott their own dances!)

So here, indeed, was a black situation for Indian dancing, a Dark Ages for Terpsichore. With the Anti-Nautch Brigade in sole command, soap-boxes creaked and groaned and caved in, the air was rent with demands for laws to forbid dancing . . . (and shouting loudest amongst them were a man and a woman of some doubtful esoteric cult who, when the dance later flowered into public esteem and favour, declared themselves to be respectively the sole performers, critics and discoverers of the art! But that is another story, and a typical one of the international world of dancing).

THE RENAISSANCE

Gradually, however, flickerings of interest in the Indian dance began to show through this wet blanket of morality and oblivion. Poet Rabindranath Tagore at Santiniketan tried to stimulate interest in 1917. In 1929, Pavlova's performances and her own interest in Indian dancing had some effect. Poet Vallathol tried his best with *Kathakali* dancers. But perhaps the most impartial, just, progressive and energetic figure, and the one who played the most important part both figuratively

33

and literally at this critical stage in the struggle for the survival of dancing and particularly of *Bharata Natya*, is that of one Mr. E. Krishna Iyer. We will, in fact, proceed to study superficially a portion of his career, which will give us a good practical idea for the violent antipathy which was felt for all Indian dancing, by Indians and Westerners alike, at that date.

At the time described, E. Krishna Iyer was a young and handsome artist in Madras. He had studied law and was bound for the High Court; but he cherished an unquenchable flame of desire to see the once sacred temple dance, *Bharata Natya*, revived and restored to its former prestige. Just visualise his task: not only was he faced by the trumpets and drums of the Anti-Nautch campaign, but also by a public engaged in cutting the wild capers prescribed by the Charleston, "Black Bottom" and "Shimmy" of the Roaring Twenties, against which the plaintive, angelic voice of the traditional veena and the insistent rhythm of the cymbals and drums of delicate *Bharata Natya* could not be heard. However, Iyer learned all he could of the dance himself, in order to be a fit prophet, and approached some young ladies of respectable birth, asking them to study this ancient dance; but his requests were misinterpreted in the worst possible way, owing to the fact that *Bharata Natya* was connected solely with *devadasis*, and they, in turn, were connected by prejudiced minds with another profession even older than dancing.

Therefore Iyer boldly decked himself up as a young woman and proceeded to perform the ancient dance himself (see Plate V). After all, he had made an exhaustive study of the technique under traditional *nattuvans*, Bharata Narainswami of Merattur in particular. He showed *Bharata Natya* in its most incisive and powerful aspect, known as the Pandanallur school, some of which is best performed by a man, and which was at that time completely unknown. After his debut, he danced anywhere where enough people could be assembled to do any good: in films, on concert platforms, at political meetings. And slowly and surely, all he said, the grace and beauty of his dance, began to leave its mark. So he moved on to his next step, and started to assemble all the remaining traditional *Bharata Natya* dancers he could find or unearth, presenting them wherever possible with a preface of his own explanation.*

Despite the tremendous prejudice and din of saxophones at that time, people began to wonder if a successful young advocate could dress as a girl, appear in public and win acclaim, there might be something in the ancient dance of India, after all? Timidly, some of the musical societies in Madras invited Iyer's prize discovery, Balasaraswathi, a young *devadasi* of great voluptuous charm and a talent which put her in a class by herself. She was a sensational success. Iyer presented Varalakshmi, a veritable dancing goddess from Kumbakonam, who had been forced to retire by the heat produced by the "Anti-Nautchers"; the Kalyani sisters, who blazed like two temple lights in the glory of the vigorous Pandanallur style.

The tremulous experiments were replaced by great competition as to which musical society could secure the best dancer, and once again large sums were

---

* That *Bharata Natya* should only be danced by women is a complete misapprehension, and a legacy from "Nautch-dance" days. To-day in South India whole *Bharata Natya* ballets are danced by men (the best performer being 74 years of age). This subject will be investigated in a later book.

PLATE V

Above: Ram Gopal in a *Bharata Natya* "padam," in which the face must speak the international language of the dance. *Left*: Srimati Jayalakshmi. Born of traditional devadasi stock, she is acknowledged in South India to be the greatest living exponent of the Pandanallur style of *Bharata Natya*.

Kumari Kamala (Madras), a leading dancer in the Valhuvlar style of *Bharata Natya*.

SRI E. KRISHNA IYER, B.A., B.L., advocate. *Left*: as he is to-day. *Right*: An historic photograph. Having failed to interest any respectable young ladies in *Bharata Natya*, when this dance style was decadent and in disrepute, Krishna Iyer performed it himself dressed as a woman. He is to-day the foremost critic and authority of this dance style in India.

PLATE VI

Janiki in a typical
Mohiniattam pose.

Ram Gopal and Chandrabhaga Devi in typical *Bharata Natya* poses. Note the clean lines of their arms.

Srimathi Balasaraswathi.

Krishna Rao and Chandrabhaga Devi
—two fine teachers of *Bharata Natya*.

Above : Kumari Kausalya, an outstanding
dancer of the Pandanallur style of *Bharata
Natya.*
Below : Rukmini Devi of Adyar.

offered to the dancers. At length a society woman in her late thirties pronounced herself ready to learn *Bharata Natya*, and Iyer took her to his teachers, concealing his amusement when he recognised in her an enthusiastic member of the bombastic Anti-Nautch campaign. She never really mastered the art, and characteristically never gave Iyer the credit due to him, taking for herself the prestige of "discovering" *Bharata Natya*, which she subsequently got all muddled up with other religious practices. Iyer knew that Terpsichore is an inscrutable goddess, and he just kept quiet, watched all that passed, and was well pleased to see that the Anti-Nautch campaign quietened down completely, and that more respectable families were beginning to patronise the great old teachers of this ancient form of the dance. His first battle had been won. He wrote profusely in all the Tamil quarterlies, papers and journals, wrote books and articles, and was in great demand as a lecturer, building up a matchless reputation as a champion of Indian art, which is increasing to this day.

One of the milestones in Iyer's early lone crusade for the revival of *Bharata Natya* was marked in 1934 when he presented his discovery, Balasaraswathi, at

AMARAVATI: 2nd century A.D. Male *flying dancers*.

APSARAS
Palampet: 12–13th cent:

Procession of male dancers + musicians (Amaravati)

JEEVARATNAM and her sister Rajalakshmi, Kalyani.

the All-India Music Conference in Benares, and gave his learned discourses on the art, which must have fallen on intelligent ears like rain on the desert.

Balasaraswathi was then a young girl, and her talent was then as it is now, something which has to be seen to be believed. She is a direct descendant in blood and in tradition of the magical sculptures of dancing. She gave special performances for Ram Gopal which I was lucky enough to attend, and the memory of her dancing is locked in my mind with a clarity which I am afraid I cannot adequately put down in prose. However, I will try to describe the first occasion on which I saw Balasaraswathi dancing.

To begin with, there was no stage as we know it: just a roof held up by bamboos, under which the Indian daylight filtered and did duty for illuminations. Balasaraswathi herself was in the simplest of costumes, and her figure statuesque, in marked contrast to the rather angular and energetic young antelopes, aspirants to *Bharata Natya*, to whom I had grown accustomed. The audience looked simple enough, but really represented a terrifying array of critics—people who were as experienced at watching *Bharata Natya* as Balasaraswathi was at performing it. With a nod of her head, she indicated to the musicians that they should begin, and raised her hands in the first pose of *Alarippu*,* the traditional opening dance.

From first to last my powers of description are inadequate to describe the miracle which took place. The impromptu stage disappeared; Balasaraswathi, a figure of Juno, disappeared also, and in her place one frescoe after another followed without a break so that one couldn't be quite sure how many people were dancing, but knew that it was an art from another world. *Jethiswaram, Shabdam, Varnam,* succeeded one another in their prescribed order, until we came to the *padams;* and as we are leaving technical explanations till later on, it will be enough to say that a *padam* may be described as a poem, or hymn, enacted by the dancer and predominated by the power of the facial expressions.

Balasaraswathi addressed herself to Ram Gopal as the guest of honour, and as I was by his side I also received full impact of this phenomenal performance. The hymn sung and played by the musicians had the traditional theme of Divine love, and this superb artiste directed all her charms at us, and we sat spellbound whilst she played with our feelings in the way which marks out the stage-genius in any land.

Perhaps her long black eyes would fix on ours unwaveringly, then it would seem as though we displeased her in some way and that she could not get away from us fast enough. When she had retired as far as possible, she seemed to debate with herself, with sidelong glances, whether after all love was not too strong a thing to be cast aside easily, and she would return to us, hesitating as if to ask forgiveness. Suddenly in the midst of the cajolings by which she seemed to try to regain our favour, she would burst into a paroxysm of contemptuous laughter, survey us with disgust, and retreat once again; only to return once more as if she would ask us, once and for all, were we false or true? to which the answer she appeared to read in our faces might move her to an exaltation of joy, or to fly to her far retreat in fear, where she would stay and cast glances at us, now timid and now mischievous—magic!

* See page 50.

NAUTCH-GIRL or
DEVADASI
from Baroda.

Late 19th century.

SIVA & PARVATI

COMBINED AS
ARDHANARI

DIPA-LAKSHMI
(Beauty-Lamp)
Madras,
Chola period
bronze, 10-13th
century A.D.

After the performance we went to deliver our thanks to Balasaraswathi. I blinked to see this rather heavy, tired, hot woman, who could so change herself at will. She had only eyes for Ram Gopal, who has learned from her teachers and whom she trusts to carry the torch of *Bharata Natya* all over the world. We left with her the little heap of gifts we had brought, and they seemed very poor after the beauty of the world she had shown us.

To return to E. Krishna Iyer. It had always been his hope that some dancer with an international reputation would appear who had sufficient skill, strength and dexterity to master the ancient classical technique of *Bharata Natya* and carry it to world-wide audiences; and when he met the young Ram Gopal in 1940—having already studied *Bharata Natya* in its gentler aspects from Elappa, Puttappa, Gouri and Muthukumaram—Iyer suggested that Ram Gopal should accompany him to Tanjore and study the ancient style in its more virile aspect, in short the Pandanallur style with its broad, sweeping movements, powerful footwork and incredible leaps. Ram Gopal was eager, and eventually took an intensive and full training, and when he emerged and gave expositions of *Bharata Natya* in public, needless to say another uproar started at once. This time it was "—— a *man* dancing *Bharata Natya*? Impossible!" and so forth.

Let it be noted here that the ancient teachers of *Bharata Natya* are full of jealously guarded traditional secrets. They will sanction all manner of written testimonials for any pupil, for a respectable fee, but *they will only tell their secrets and teach all they know to their favourites—i.e.,* those whom they consider spiritually capable of learning this ancient art, as well as financially capable. Let it be remarked furthermore that these elderly gentlemen are all performers themselves and that therefore they fail to see anything peculiar in male pupils. And to Ram Gopal they taught all they knew.

It is only natural, then, that when Ram Gopal appeared armed with his con-

ANCIENT TEMPLE-DANCER & MUSICIANS: KHAJURAHO, CIRCA 10ᵗʰ·11 CENT. A.D.
(bas-relief).

siderable stage experience and fame, and in addition a very thorough knowledge of *Bharata Natya*, he was immediately recognised as a deadly rival by every woman performer (if one excepts Balasaraswathi and the real *devadasis*, who hailed him as an equal); and in proportion to his public success, the reproofs from the ladies grew angrier and angrier. They made it clear that they considered *Bharata Natya* should only be performed by themselves; and this tirade continues to this very day, the chorus being swelled by some of Ram Gopal's own lady pupils whom he trained after learning the art himself. Those elderly teachers' reluctance to teach everything to everybody is therefore doubly understandable. I include this example of jealousy as a corrective to those Westerners who believe that all Indian dancing is performed in an atmosphere of pious sanctity, and that envy and hatred is the sole prerogative of *ballets russe*.

Before we leave the subject of *Bharata Natya* as it may be seen in India to-day and set about technical details, a short account of this dance performed in a temple, as was originally intended, will not come amiss. The scene is set in Belur, Mysore State, with the indescribable temple itself providing the decor; the lighting comes from burning oil in lamps made of shining brass; the time, evening; the scent, an intoxicating mixture of jasmine, stephanotis and incense; the orchestra sits around as only Indian musicians know how, calmly expectant. The audience is composed, not of city critics as before, but of villagers, intellectuals, *devadasis* and their teachers—people, in fact, who know their dancing inside out and won't miss a thing. Every detail of the performance they will watch out of their long, black eyes; young and old, there is no hoodwinking them; they can't be dazzled into overlooking an alien movement, nor will you find them taking the trouble to turn out to watch some society beauty or subsidised amateur struggling, as a publicity-stunt, with steps, gestures and expressions which are second nature to them, the members of the audience. They had come to watch the finer subtleties of performance, and if I had been the dancer I should have died with apprehension. As it was, the performer was Ram Gopal.

As we have seen, Indian dancing and particularly the ideal *Bharata Natya* school is devotional in character. The purely rhythmic items, such as *Alarippu*, are dedicated to the presiding deity of the temple—but they also serve to give the spectator a chance to sum up the dancer's technical ability and style. Later on, when the descriptive and invocational dances begin, the audience, in following the dancer with their senses and sympathy, contribute to the general atmosphere of devotion; any philistine present will have an unhappy evening as he won't understand what is going on, but that is his affair. So the audience, the majority of which knows countless legends concerning each god, settles down first to watch the dancer prove himself technically; and then, as in this case, see how, in the course of a *padam* he will tell a legend of the mischievous Blue God, Sri Krishna.

CONTEMPORARY DANCER & MUSICIANS: SRIMATI BALASARASWATHI, MADRAS, 20ᵗʰ CENT:

Tambura
Cymbals (or talam) & Natuvanar (or singer)
Veena
Mrdangam
Balasaraswathi

And this is where the miracle happens again. The dancer can *become* Sri Krishna under one's very eyes.

It is true that the dancer is flesh and blood, for a short while ago he was dancing as a technical virtuoso and there he is, still in the same costume. He hasn't paused to take any stimulant or to rest, and the *mis-en-scène* is exactly as it was. He has certainly great physical charm—but where did he get this unearthly beauty? How does he flash about, sometimes gliding, sometimes covering immense distances with a single leap, pausing only in poses of indescribable dignity, and then as suddenly melting into the Divine mischievousness of the irrepressible god, teasing the villagers, upsetting the village maids, stealing milk and butter; to end in the favourite pose of Krishna, legs crossed, the flute at his lips, and lively, slanting black eyes still on the look-out for celestial fun.

The *devadasis* know that this transfiguration is a rare thing and they lie there never moving, their long eyes narrowed and never missing a single detail. The musicians play as if enchanted. The audience knows, and the old teachers know, that the Blue God is not only living but before their eyes. Afterwards they will confer and nod gravely together, and the villagers will look at each other and smile. Ram Gopal may ask you "How was it?" with perfect modesty, but the odds are you will be quite speechless.

     .   .   .   .   .

A great stage personality and dancer must also have powers of *transfiguration*, which means that he must also be a great creative artist. And a Western audience which has seen the performance of Ram Gopal has a double shock to survive— first, that the man turns into a god, and back into a man; and second, the Indian scene which he creates at will turns back again into our own familiar stage. That is the magic of stage genius, in comparison with which the most polished conjuror can only appear a limited and clumsy illusionist.

In conclusion, it may be affirmed that the dance-art of *Bharata Natya* from the depths of violent social prejudice, has now ascended the wobbly step-ladder to social fame. If you are presenting a programme of dances in India, you must include a little *Bharata Natya;* in consequence the qualities of the present dancers of the age-old style range from a bombastic and self-assertive exaggeration of the original technique, through a dull, uninteresting over-academic style, to an undulating, sexy, softened and altogether repugnant version which is artistically worse than the original eroticism which had until recently cost *Bharata Natya* its social prestige; for the genuine *devadasis*, even if they transgressed the laws of contemporary society, at least made seduction into a fine art, whereas the charlatans of the present day have resorted to lewd looks and gestures which are more suggestive of back-streets after midnight than of the courtship of an *apsaras*. In other words, *Bharata Natya* is in danger again.

THE ARRANGEMENT OF THE CONTEMPORARY PROGRAMME OF *BHARATA NATYA*

In the traditional schools of South India, and for public performances to-day, *Bharata Natya* survives in the form of the programme set down at the end of this section. Amongst other survivals of this classic dance which have not been transported on to the public stage are the South Indian *Kuruvanji* ballets, in which a number of performers combine to invoke the gods and enact mythological events, on the scale of the *Kathakali* dance-drama of Malabar, but inside the temple instead of outside; of course, using the traditional *Bharata Natya* technique, mudras and expressions. Performed in the month of April, these ballets are considered to be the nearest approach to the sacred ballets described in the *Natya Śastras* as enacted at the time of its composition, and for thousands of years until the present day. There are also extremely esoteric dances performed on religious occasions by the priests themselves.

It must be strongly emphasised that *Bharata Natya* in its true and proper form should be studied in the manner stipulated by the Hindus, as one of the *Sastras* which it is, and at the feet of a recognised *guru* or master, who performs the ceremony of his pupil's initiation and thereafter fulfils the function of spiritual as well as physical instructor. The reasons are too obvious to be enumerated here.

The programme below, and the sketches of steps which follow give no indication of the immense and arduous training to be undergone by the serious student of *Bharata Natya* in connection with the control of expression, facial mobility, traditional gestures and so forth. A deep knowledge of mythology must also be learned—and felt—by the student. To dance invocations to gods of whom one has no real knowledge and sympathy is not only sacrilegious, but artistically useless, rather like studying meaningless gymnastics in order to become a poet; but I believe that to glance through the sequences of sketches will give some impression of the clean lines, virility, agility, and lightness which together with the powerful footwork mark the genuine *Bharata Natya* dancer, and will give the lie to the suave understatements of the "softened-up" film or society dancer, and the heavy overstatements of the amateur.

The purely technical ingredients for a physical mastery of *Bharata Natya* are: swiftness, precision, suppleness, strength (for endurance!), an irreproachable instinct for time and rhythm, agility, and lightness. But what the South Indian experts look for, above all, is an expressive face, or inner emotion expressed in an outward and clearly visible form. This is an attribute which has marked all the great artist-dancers in history, but is regarded as a gift of nature in the West; in South India however, this facial expressiveness is understood, sought for, cultivated and acclaimed to a degree unknown elsewhere.

The following arrangement of a recital of *Bharata Natya*, it should be noted, is not claimed to be an exact reproduction of any ancient curriculum given in the *Natya Sastras*, any more than a contemporary performance of ballet as we know it in the West is supposed to deliver an exact reproduction of 17th century ballet as danced in the French palaces.

It is however accepted by the foremost critics and intelligentsia in South India as the best arrangement for a contemporary solo performance, as it has been devised by masters each of whom are recognised descendants of the direct line of the Tanjore classical *Bharata Natya* dance school.

An entire recital or solo performance of *Bharata Natya* is composed of the following items, given in order of their performance:

1. ALARIPPU   4. VARNAM

2. JETHISWARAM 5. PADAM(S)

3. SHABDAM   6. THILLANA

It is reasonable to say that a full programme of *Bharata Natya* by a solo performer can take anything from an hour and a half to four hours.

BHARATA NATYA: TECHNICAL SKETCHES

COSTUME AND DEPORTMENT

The question of the modern costume most suitable for *Bharata Natya* has been raised earlier in this chapter, and by the time the reader has studied the ancient sculptures and compared them with the bundled-up costume as now generally worn (as shown in the three views of the girl in sketch E opposite) he will have discovered that the costume shown below, as designed by Ram Gopal and worn here by himself and a partner are far nearer the original, classical lines. As to the question of modesty—Marco Polo says of the temple dancers "those girls . . . dance and sing, all but naked, in front of the god and goddess . . ." and it may be noted that modesty isn't always a matter of covering one's figure. The sketch of Mohini (sketch D) is more modest than the modern creation shown in sketch F, although it is more naked. A *choli*, or classical blouse, with some sort of draped trouser is the correct costume (see Jain dancer, p. 7). Incidentally, the beautiful

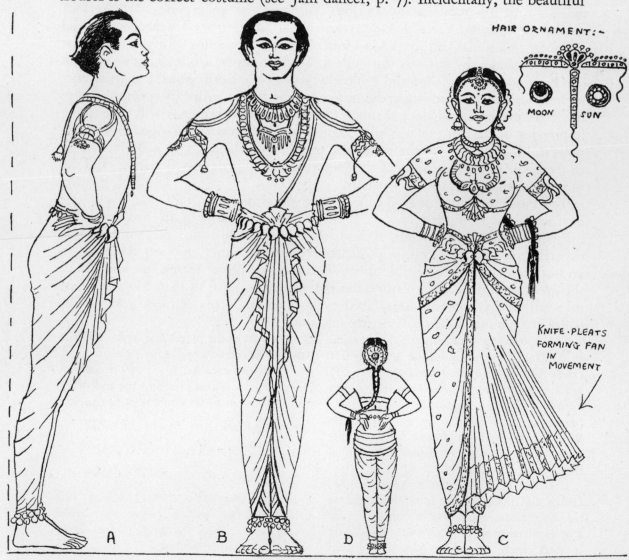

HAIR ORNAMENT:—

MOON SUN

KNIFE-PLEATS
FORMING FAN
IN
MOVEMENT

A   B   D   C

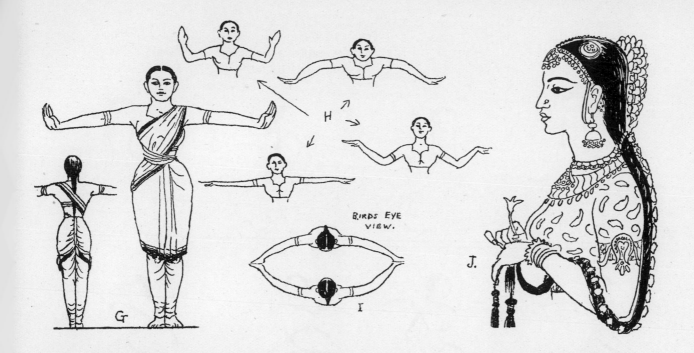

BIRDS EYE VIEW.

classical jewellery and ornamentation comes from Tanjore, the preserve of the ancient dance-style itself.

The basic stance for *Bharata Natya* as shown by Ram Gopal, and the carriage of the arms as shown above in sketches **G** and **I** are in accordance with the best and most practical rules of all physical deportment, and will be found to correspond with the best academic style of posture prescribed by *ballet russe*, with the elbows always supported and the whole carriage of the body pitched slightly forward from heels to chin. The bundled-up young lady has it all wrong—that is *Kathakali* stance, not *Bharata Natya*.

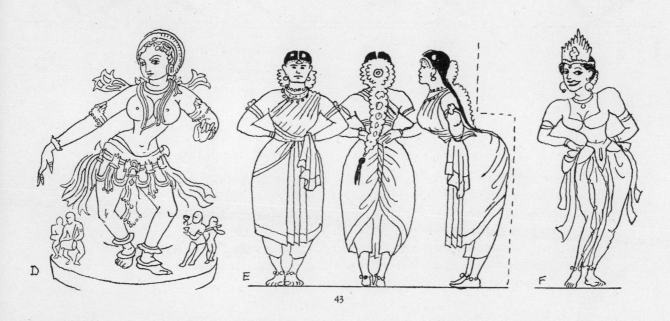

(N.B.: The KATHAKALI names for hand-gestures are often different or contrary to the following BHARATA NATYA designations.)

A

B 1   2   3

COUNT: and — — — — — — — one

HASTA PATAKA   TAIPATAKA

C
1   2   3   4

COUNT:

5   6   7   8   9   REPEAT WHOLE SEQUENCE OTHER SIDE

PRELIMINARY EXERCISES AND SIMPLE STEPS, OR *ADAVUS*

Here is a private view of Ram Gopal's studio in Bangalore, South India. The little girl at the top of the page is learning to use her feet and Ram Gopal is holding her at the waist to see that she develops power and doesn't use her foot-muscles only, but the weight of her own body. He teaches her the rhythmical "shoulder-movement", a knack which is tricky at first, as pupils tend to exaggerate it. The jumping exercise is to give elasticity and accustom the dancer to the low bend in which so many of the dances are performed.

44

SHOULDER-MOVEMENT:
Practise thus:—

PULL!

— keeping body
straight &
facing front.

C.

WARMING-UP
EXERCISE:—
small jumps
in this position

D.

THE HAND-GESTURES USED
ON THESE TWO PAGES:

HASTA-
PATAKA

TRIPATAKA

ALAPADMA

E   1
COUNT:

2
THAI

3
THAI
LAPADMA

4
DI

5
DI

6
THAI

REPEAT
SEQUENCE
OTHER
SIDE.

ANCIENT SCULPTURES
ARE THE BEST GUIDE
TO MOVEMENT.

On right,
dancer from
BELUR (12th century.)

The simple sequences of steps, as those shown in C and E above, are usually performed as an exercise, first slowly and then double-time. *Absolute precision is essential* whether the time is slow or fast. For future reference: an *adavu* is a simple step or basic movement, as shown here, and may be compared, in ballet, to a classroom exercise or step. An *adavu-jethi* is a combination of *adavus* and may be compared to an *enchaînement* in the ballet. A *thirmanam* is a sequence of pure rhythmic dance composed of *adavu-jethis* and may be compared to a ballet *variation*. It is in the execution of *thirmanams* that the technical virtuosity, timing and rhythmic sense of the *Bharata Natya* dancer shows itself.

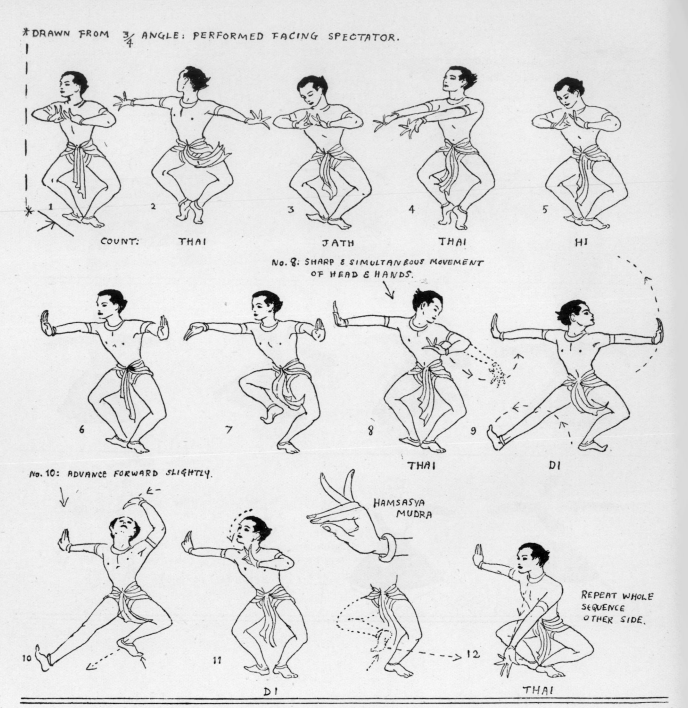

*DRAWN FROM ¾ ANGLE: PERFORMED FACING SPECTATOR.

COUNT: THAI   JATH   THAI   HI

No. 8: SHARP & SIMULTANEOUS MOVEMENT OF HEAD & HANDS.

THAI   DI

No. 10: ADVANCE FORWARD SLIGHTLY.

HAMSASYA MUDRA

REPEAT WHOLE SEQUENCE OTHER SIDE.

DI   THAI

AN *ADAVU-JETHI*

Here we have two separate steps combined, as described on the previous page. Again the dancer would be judged on his precision. His footwork must be neither blurred, nor over-emphasised; and in the course of this sequence, which is performed at a considerable speed, his head, arms and hands must be as swift and clearly marked as the rhythm he beats with his feet. Incidentally, although the dancer must wear bells round his ankles for a stage performance, he must practise without them.

HAMSASYA HANDS

ALAPADMA

SIKHARA MUDRA

TRIPATAKA

THIS SEQUENCE IS PERFORMED SIDEWAYS THUS:

AN EXAMPLE OF ELEVATION IN *BHARATA NATYA* :
ANOTHER *ADAVU-JETHI*

Here is a specimen of one of those leaps which your teacher will tell you must be as effortless as an antelope, as light as a feather and as high as the sky. It is performed sideways, but is only one example of elevation in *Bharata Natya*. Demonstrated by Ram Gopal, I have seen him cover the length of a full temple corridor in three such leaps, coming forward. To land with a crash is emphatically tabu. The words which are spoken by the *nattuvan* to accompany pure dance are indicated on some of these sketches (*e.g.,* on the left, *thaijath thaihi thai di di thai*) are an integral part of the performance. What we should call the basic beat is left to the instinct of the dancer. Ram Gopal calls the chant "winged words."

47

CORRECT METHOD (*Allegro Vivace*).—

← 4: BOTH HANDS ALAPADMA

HAMSASYA   ALAPADMA

A. 1   2   3   4   5   REPEAT OTHER SIDE

| FAST TIME: | THAI - JATH | | THAI - HI | THAI - JATH | THAI - HI (etc.) |
| COUNT: | AND | 1 | AND | 2 | AND | 3 | AND | 4 | AND (etc.) |

INCORRECT METHOD (*into battle!*):—
(*Compare with sketches above.*)

B. 1   2   3   4   5   NEVER REPEAT !!

WARNINGS

To master the technique of *Bharata Natya* it is not only necessary to learn to control every muscle, but *an intelligent and sympathetic study of the character of the dance itself* is also indispensable and especially if the student has not the inherited qualities of the dance inborn, as for example the great Balasaraswathi. Even excluding the dances in which *abhinaya* (facial expression) are featured, it is easy to make fundamental mistakes of style and taste in the approach to the *nrtta* (pure dance) aspect.

To clarify this point, in sequence A above Ram Gopal shows a typical *adavu-iethi*, with the requisite precision, delicacy and underlying power. Sequence B shows a girl who believes that pure energy is superior to anything else. With thunderous stamping and an expression of grim determination, ornaments whizzing in all directions, her performance is an ordeal for all concerned. C, below, shows the same degree of error, but understatement this time instead of overstatement.

On the right: an *adavu-jethi* featuring a beautiful twist of the spine, strongly reminiscent of the dancing-girls of the sculptures. 9a shows the inevitable distortion, and that awful costume. Jasmine-flowers should also be worn with a certain reserve.

INCORRECT METHOD
C.

COMPARE WITH FIGS. 25-26 IN FOLLOWING "ALARIPPU"

48

TRIPATAKA

SIKHARA HANDS

6 - 8 :-
3 STEPS
ROUND TO
FACE BACK
START WITH
R FOOT.

5

Shoulder movement

4

3

2

1

6, 7 & 8:
HAMSASYA HANDS

ALAPADMA HANDS

6

7

MIRROR

8

9.

9A
AN OFTEN SEEN &
INCORRECT VERSION
OF N° 9.

BELOW
TIME OF THIS SEQUENCE (L. foot first.) 4 bars of 4 beats

COUNT: 1   2   3-4   1-2   3   4

1   2   3-4   1   2   3   4

9 - 11: 4 STEPS
TO FACE FRONT.
(L-R, L-R.)
REPEAT OTHER
SIDE

HAMSASYA HANDS

TRIPATAKA HAND

11

10

49

TISRAM ALARIPPU

There are two *Alarippus*, *tisram* and *misram*, as previously described. The following sketches show the entire arrangement of the *tisram Alarippu*, as taught by Meenakshisundaram Pillai of the Pandanallur school, and arranged by Ram Gopal for two performers. The partner—a girl in this case—is only sketched when her movements differ from the man's. Each movement is sketched once only but by a solo performer is usually executed first to the right. The rhythms and tempos can only be suggested. *Alarippu* is always performed first at a recital of *Bharata Natya* and is danced in an invocational spirit. Compared to some of the items which succeed it, it is simple to perform; but the cunningly built-up climax and the wonderful balance of time, movement and speeds with the juxtaposition of body, feet, head and limbs makes it a test of the dancer's elegance, dignity and taste. Figs. 1–6 are the obeisance to Siva, without which no performance may begin, or no class take place.

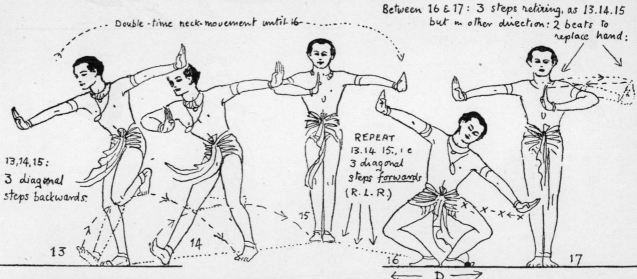

* The Alarippu begins with a rhythmical movement of the neck, which there is no room to describe here.

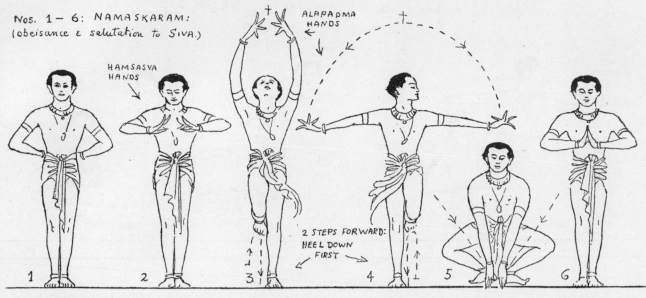

Nos. 1 — 6: NAMASKARAM:
(obeisance & salutation to SIVA.)

HAMSASYA HANDS

ALAPADMA HANDS

2 STEPS FORWARD: HEEL DOWN FIRST

1   2   3   4   5   6

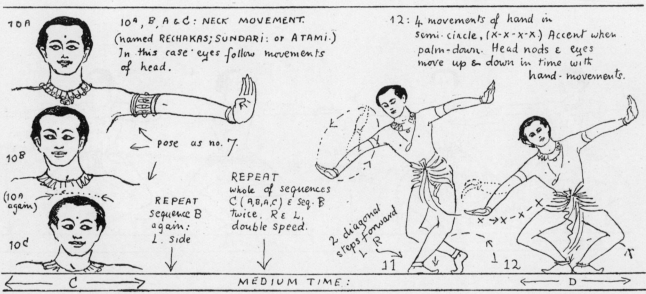

10ᴬ

10ᴬ, B, A & C: NECK MOVEMENT.
(named RECHAKAS; SUNDARI: or ATAMI.)
In this case eyes follow movements of head.

12: 4 movements of hand in semi-circle, (X-X-X-X) Accent when palm-down. Head nods & eyes move up & down in time with hand-movements.

10ᴮ

← pose as no. 7.

(10ᴬ again)

10ᶜ

REPEAT sequence B again: L. side

REPEAT whole of sequences C (A,B,C) & Seq. B twice. R & L, double speed.

2 diagonal steps forward L R

11   12

x → x - x - x

←——— C ———→   MEDIUM TIME: ←——— D ———→

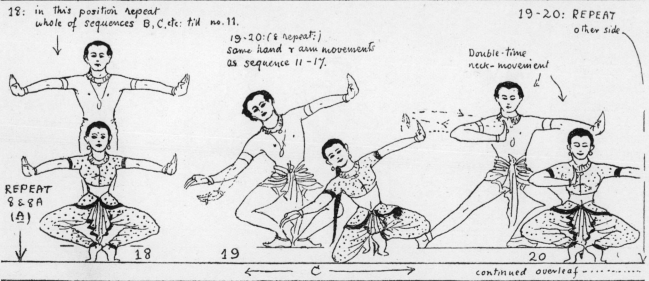

18: in this position repeat whole of sequences B, C etc: till no. 11.

19-20: REPEAT other side.

19-20: (& repeat:) same hand & arm movements as sequence 11-17.

Double-time neck-movement

REPEAT 8 & 8A (A)

18   19   20

←——— C ———→   continued overleaf - - - - - - - - -

E: REPEAT
twice R. side
twice L. side.

Then: E once
F once } R. side, & E once
F once } L. side

TRIPATAKA
HANDS

ALAPADMA
HANDS

21   22   23

←— — — — — — — E — — →   Shoot knee forward — — →   ←— — — — — F

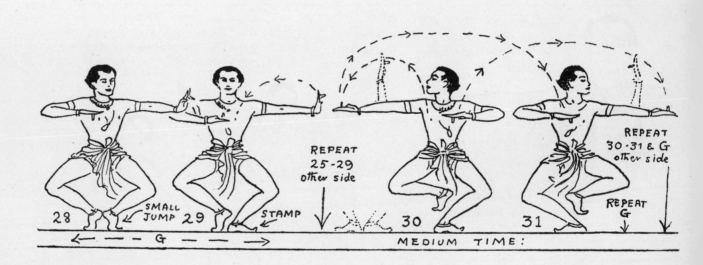

REPEAT
25-29
other side

REPEAT
30·31 & G
other side

REPEAT
G

28   SMALL
JUMP   29   STAMP   30   31

←— — — G — — — →   MEDIUM TIME:

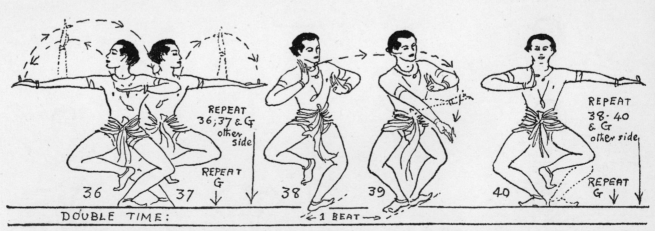

REPEAT
36;37 & G
other
side

REPEAT
G

REPEAT
38· 40
& G
other side,

REPEAT
G

36   37   38   39   40

DOUBLE TIME: ←— 1 BEAT —→

52

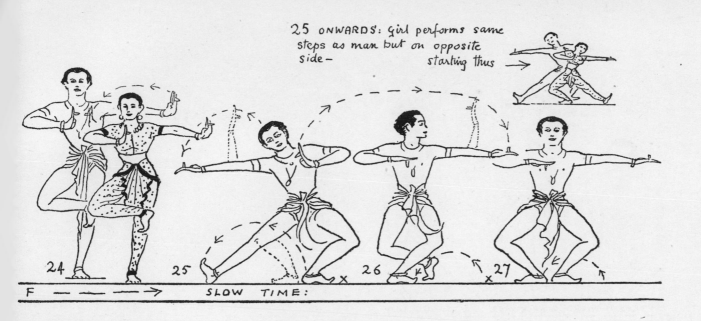

25 ONWARDS: Girl performs same steps as man but on opposite side — starting thus →

24   25   SLOW TIME: 26   27

F — — — →   SLOW TIME:

32   33   34   35

PIVOT L. FOOT   PIVOT R. FOOT

REPEAT 32-35 & G other side

REPEAT G

41   42   REPEAT H   43   44   REPEAT H: feet as below   45   REPEAT H: feet as below

← H →   continued overleaf ·········

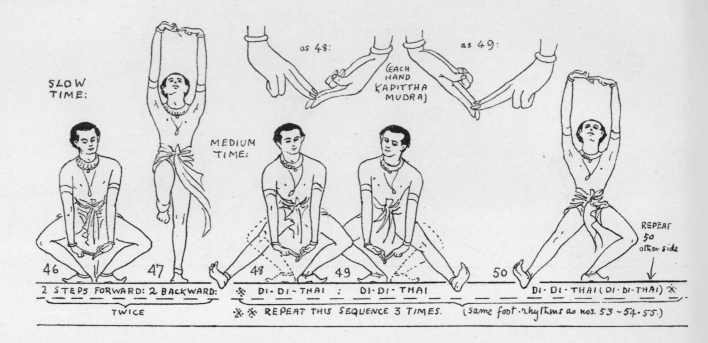

SLOW TIME:

MEDIUM TIME:

as 48:

(EACH HAND KAPITTHA MUDRA)

as 49:

REPEAT 50 other side

46   47   48   49   50

2 STEPS FORWARD: 2 BACKWARD: ✳ DI-DI-THAI : DI-DI-THAI   DI-DI-THAI (DI-DI-THAI) ✳

TWICE   ✳✳ REPEAT THIS SEQUENCE 3 TIMES.   (same foot rhythms as nos. 53·54·55.)

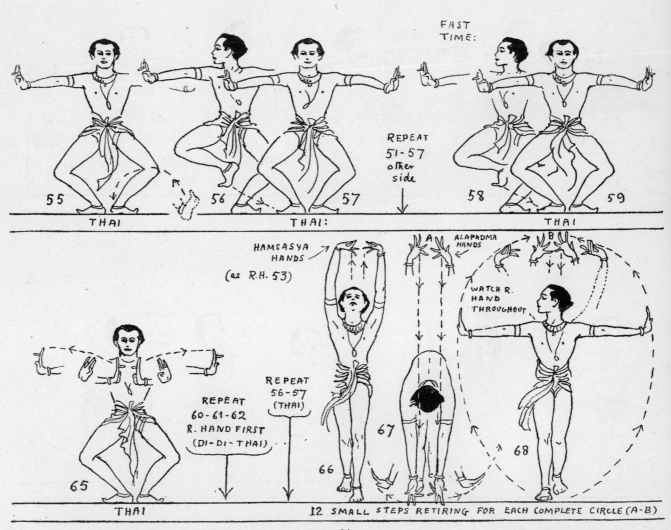

FAST TIME:

REPEAT 51-57 other side

55   56   57   58   59

THAI   THAI: THAI

HAMSASYA HANDS

(as R.H. 53)

A   ALAPADMA HANDS   B

WATCH R. HAND THROUGHOUT

REPEAT 56-57 (THAI)

REPEAT 60-61-62 R. HAND FIRST (DI-DI-THAI)

65   66   67   68

THAI   12 SMALL STEPS RETIRING FOR EACH COMPLETE CIRCLE (A-B)

ALAPADMA
HAND

HAMSASYA
MUDRA

51 THAI
52 THAI
53 DI-
54 DI-

SIDE
VIEWS

60 61

BIRD'S EYE VIEWS: 63 64

60 DI-
61 DI-

L. FOOT
ADVANCES
SLIGHTLY

62 THAI:

60·61·62:
same
feet
as
53·54·55.

63 THAI
64 THAI

XA:
REPEAT
60·61·62 L. SIDE
(DI· DI· THAI)

XB:
REPEAT
63·64
R HAND FIRST
(THAI, THAI)

XA XB

FINAL CIRCLE

REPEAT
66·67·68
UNTIL TWO WHOLE
CIRCLES WITH THE HANDS
HAVE BEEN COMPLETED.
I.E. 24 STEPS BACKWARDS

2 STEPS
FOREWARDS

69

NECK MOVEMENT
ONCE, R - L.

70. FINIS.

SLOW TIME:

55

figs. 1-6: BOTH HANDS
TRIPATAKA

X ①   ②   ③   ④ X

SONG: "THUS DANCED

HANDS COMBINED:
ABHAYA MUDRA

PATAKA
HANDS

⑪

⑫

13: TAKE THIS POSE ON
FLAT OF RIGHT FOOT. &
RISE ON ¾ POINT TWICE

⑬

"SO, HE DANCES"

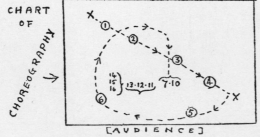

CHART OF CHOREOGRAPHY →

[AUDIENCE]

NATANAM ADINAR: *Lord Śiva's Cosmic Dance of Creation.*
Performed to an ecstatic and beautiful hymn to Śiva, it
is one of the most virile and exhausting male solos
imaginable: Time six minutes.

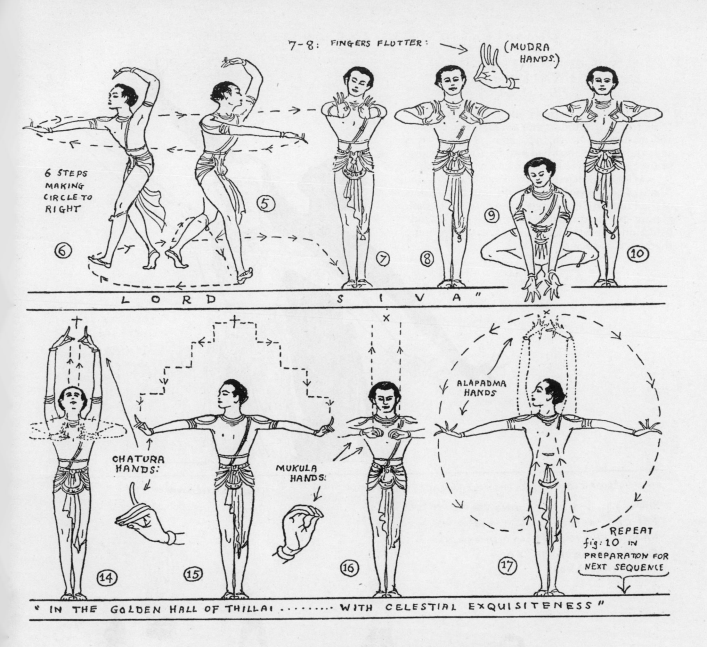

7-8: FINGERS FLUTTER: → (MUDRA HANDS.)

6 STEPS MAKING CIRCLE TO RIGHT

⑥ ⑤

⑦ ⑧ ⑨ ⑩

" L O R D   S I V A "

CHATURA HANDS:

MUKULA HANDS:

ALAPADMA HANDS

REPEAT fig: 10 IN PREPARATION FOR NEXT SEQUENCE

⑭ ⑮ ⑯ ⑰

" IN THE GOLDEN HALL OF THILLAI .... WITH CELESTIAL EXQUISITENESS "

PADAMS: THE FIRST SEQUENCE FROM *NATANAM ADINAR*

Because the scale of these sketches is small, I have chosen a dance-sequence which is more remarkable for action than for the delicacy of its facial expressions —in some ways a pity as Ram Gopal has a face which is second to none for showing shades of feeling, for which talent many *padams* give him full scope.

I selected *Natanam Adinar* because Ram Gopal's performance of this vigorous dance has given it a popularity which has led many ladies to attempt to perform it, whereas Lord Siva as he creates the world is not a subject suitable for a woman performer. On p. 19 there is a sketch of the *Natarajah*, or Siva as Lord of the Dance, and the pose will be recognised here in Fig. 13. The hymns featuring Divine love are matchless when interpreted by a girl; unfortunately space does not permit me to include an example here.

THE FINAL ITEM IN THE CONTEMPORARY
BHARATA NATYA PROGRAMME;
THILLANA

The *Tarana*, a form of song, came to South India from the Hindusthani *ustads*, music teachers and masters of North India about 150–200 years ago, and became absorbed into the Carnatic music of the South, where it is now known as a *Thillana*. It was incorporated as a dance-form in the *Bharata Natya* programme by the four late masters of the Ponniah Pillai family, who taught it to their present-day descendants. It consists of a melody based on 8 beats, with the dancer performing rhythmical variations.

A CHARACTERISTIC MOVEMENT FROM THE THILLANA RECALLING THE ANCIENT FRESCOES & FRIEZES

AN INDICATION OF THE GENERAL CHOREOGRAPHY OF THE THILLANA.
Below, figs. 1–6: 8 GLIDING STEPS IN CRESCENT-PATTERN, REPEATED 4 TIMES.
HANDS CHANGE FROM HAMSASYA TO ALAPADMA WITH EACH STEP THROUGHOUT.

ALAPADMA HANDS

HAMSASYA HANDS

A U D I E N C E

PLATE VII

Cecil Beaton

Ram Gopal rehearses with his *Natuvanar* on the sea-shore near Bombay: a photographic record by Cecil Beaton which future dancers will study, just as Ram Gopal studies the records of the Ajanta painters to-day.

PLATE VIII

Above: A present-day "Trimurti" of the dance. (*Left*) Kunju Kurup, an actor-dancer-mime to-day. Over 60, he still takes part in the traditional 16-hour dance-dramas. He taught Ram Gopal all he knew of *Kathakali.* (*Centre*) Meenakshi Sundaram Pillai, the grand old man of the Pandanallur school of *Bharata Natya.* (*Right*) Ram Gopal, their devoted pupil.

Left : *Kathakali* is a friendly technique and can be used to express any idea. Here Ram Gopal and partner dance as Śiva and Parvati, using as a basis *Kathakali* technique.

Left : Ram Gopal in the *Cobra Devil Dance*—an exciting excerpt from *Kathakali* dance-drama.

Right : An action-picture of Ram Gopal as *King Rugmangada* in meditation. For touring, the traditional rice-paste make-up, which takes so many hours to apply, has to be replaced with a " ready-made " chin of india-rubber.

CORONATION OF
RAMA: FROM A
MURAL, COCHIN.
(Probably painted
circa 16 - 17ᵗʰ cent
A/D, but some
examples go
back to 9ᵗʰ cent:)

CHAPTER IV

*KATHAKALI**

NOTES ON HISTORY AND BACKGROUND OF *KATHAKALI*

One of the principal features of Indian history is that in its earlier stages there are few "dates", which makes things difficult for the document-loving mind. History was certainly made very vigorously, with terrific battles, kings were murdered, deposed, thrones usurped, laws made and broken, empires came and went, but there were no historians to sit in a safe place and make records, and we rely on chance diaries of stray monks and travellers for information of splendid lost cities, and on private letters and the like for battles which shook the whole sub-continent. As for the ordinary people—they just went on looking for *bhuts*

* *Katha* meaning "story", *Kali* meaning "play": thus "story-play" or "danced-drama".

(ghosts) round their huts every night, hoping for a good harvest, and didn't give unnecessary attention to politics. They had always had and would always have to pay taxes to someone: what did it matter to whom?

Artistic history is a different matter. It is hard, looking at an historic boundary-line, to tell just when it was moved, and how; but to look at a sculpture can be a matter of pedigree—North Indian lyrical symmetry, South Indian genius nurtured on ecstatic religious devotion; indigenous arts mixed with Egyptian, Greek, Mohammedan arts—and not always in a conquering spirit either, but sometimes in a spirit of fraternal and tolerant artistry. In the West, we may rely on the dates of kings to tell us when a cathedral was built; in India, very often it is the artistic style of the architecture which tells us the date of the king.

From the time that the document-conscious settlers from Europe and other lands started to arrive in India in numbers in their various capacities as traders, stake-claimers and so forth, Indian history begins to boast regular dates—with the result that many dangerously bad mistakes are made concerning the antiquity of art-forms and especially dancing. Some people are misled into believing that the *Kathak* dance of North India only started with Maharaj Binda Din, simply because he was the first to write it down. And I have read as an actual preface to a dance-programme, supposed to instruct the world in *Kathakali* dancing, that this dance "came into existence in the 16th century in Malabar." At this rate *Kathakali* would be no older than the Western academic ballet technique; and one has only to use ones eyes and wits to perceive that this dance style is far older than that.

For two thousand years there has been an almost unbroken tradition of theatrical arts in Kerala (old Malabar) where an "artist caste" was created to ensure continuity; the members of the caste were maintained by gifts of land and rations at the expense of suitable authorities, giving their services in return, when required—the ideal arrangement of a subsidy, given in those days by rajah, king or art-loving nobleman, and supplied in modern times by the state, as in Russia, France, Finland, Denmark and England.

The benevolent, indigenous religious system of South Travancore made the character of the people readily absorbent towards foreign art. Punam Nambudiri, a composer in Malayālam gives us a clue to *his* date when he tells of the arrival of people for the festival of Rama's coronation—wearing Portuguese hats.

The mention of Rama, the gentle, perfect knight of Indian mythology, brings us to the famous Cochin murals, an example of which appears at the head of this chapter. Compare it with the sketch of Ram Gopal as King Rugmangada on p. 65. The similarity is obvious and striking: what is the main difference? The mural shows King Rama *in a dhoti*, the classical Indian trouser, and with a bare torso. Ram Gopal, preparing for a contemporary sixteen-hour performance, wears the costume invariably used to-day, featuring a thick woollen or cotton jacket coloured red (or yellow or green) and a *crinoline-like billowing skirt*. In all other respects, headdress, jewellery, etc., the costume is precisely the same. In the continuation of the mural Sita is represented dressed similarly to her husband, with the upper part of her body bare. To-day, the female dancers must also wear the jacket.

Now if those additions weren't caused by the Portuguese and/or Dutch residents of that time we may eat our hats. One may logically assume that the Portuguese and/or Dutch ladies and reverend gentlemen fainted dead away at the very idea of exposed female bosoms and even male ones; and that the twenty-four white layers of skirts were probably affected in accordance with the attire of the contemporary European ladies, along with the cumbersome, hot, long-sleeved jackets, as gestures of friendship and Western decency, as the kings and rajahs of Malabar wisely made it their policy to try to avoid trouble with their visitors, to save their people from the horrors of militant instead of peaceful invasion.

The costumes shown in the frescœ are perfect for dancing: the subsequent addition of thick jackets covering torso and arms and billowing skirts is not only obviously unsuitable for that hot climate, but encumbers the dancer. The facial expressions are purest *Kathakali* as cultivated to-day—but in the course of actual performances at the present time one notices the right hand of the actor-dancer hold his head-dress, which has grown enormous, in position as he performs a swift passage of the dance: in spite of which precaution the huge superstructure sometimes ruins the elaborate make-up of the performer, which it dislodges at the forehead and cheeks.

In common with ancient *Bharata Natya*, and also the Western ballets which were performed in his palaces by a French king, *Kathakali* was often distinguished by royalty on the cast of its performers, rajahs and monarchs being justly proud to take part in the dance-dramas.

Lastly, it may be noted that in the real *Kathakali* dance-dramas of to-day, girls and women are not permitted to take part as it is considered too virile, difficult and lengthy for them. Some young women of ungainly proportions, attempting to perform *Kathakali* to-day in its masculine aspect with more energy than taste, are said by the great dance-masters to portend evil and warn of disaster!

THE PRESENT DAY DANCE-DRAMA

In the course of these very necessary enquiries into the background and evolution of dancing one is apt to overlook present day realities. Therefore a brief glimpse of a contemporary performance of a *Kathakali* dance-drama will not be out of place.

If you lived in Malabar with its feathery palm-trees, graceful, composed inhabitants and brooding air of antiquity, you might suddenly hear a great deal of gong-sounding and drum-beating from the nearest Kerala temple—a bell-shaped building fantastically decorated inside and out. You could discover that this portentous clamour advertised to all within earshot (a considerable radius!) that there was to be a performance of a dance-drama the following night, which would start at dusk and continue in all probability for sixteen hours.

A migration then starts towards the temple and of course, you would join it. Your companions would include whole families, complete with beds for everyone and milk for the baby, making their dusky-eyed way on foot; families in bullock-carts, horse-carts, hand-carts, and motor-cars of suitable antiquity, all piled, bulging and overflowing with people; later on, perhaps a few Daimlers containing the local aristocracy. Everyone makes himself at home in the court outside the temple, the older ones bribing the younger ones to wake them at the moment their favourite actor or episode takes place. The discussions before, throughout and after the performance are exactly similar to those of dance enthusiasts all over the world, furious partisanship, comparing this dancer with that, with the elderly people complaining that the standard was far higher in their day.

The daylight starts to fade and the huge oil-lamp is lit—two men are specially engaged to feed it with oil and resin throughout the performance—and this will serve as stage-lighting, sometimes flanked by torches as well. Actors and dancers approach the light when they are to enact special passages, much as the lime-light singles out details and personalities in the Western theatre.

The night eventually becomes peopled with strange and shadowy beings, gods, demons, half-man half beast, hunters and veiled ladies. The performance will deal with events that shattered the three worlds, and looking at the personnel we are prepared to believe it. The basic moral is always that of the eternal warfare between Good and Evil.

Just imagine the effect of the eventual appearance of Ravana, the Demon King, in such a setting. The flames leap in the brass burner with the brooding outlines of the temple dimly seen in the background. A brilliantly coloured cloth is held near the brass lamp by two attendants, as high as their arms can stretch, and violent drumming warns us that a terrific personality is about to appear. The sound of quick and heavy footsteps can be heard from behind the curtain, which is violently agitated from time to time as though some nucleus of fearful power was gathering its forces on the other side. A coloured canopy magically appears from nowhere over the curtain, from behind which a rumbling growl grows to a hair-raising shriek which rises above the thunder of the drums. Before our now starting eyes, two hands, one with beautiful long silver nails, now grip the top of the violently agitated curtain, and breathless we catch an occasional glimpse of the top of a golden headdress which seems to be gyrating madly in some infernal whirlwind. What a height above the ground ——! We can't help a sidelong glance at our companions for reassurance . . . has something unforeseen occurred, have the performers gone too far in their invocations and accidentally, horribly, produced the real thing—terrible Ravana, the ten-headed with twenty arms, the invincible, destructive and evil . . . ?

And so this hellish peep-show develops. The curtain is raised, lowered and raised again until excitement reaches fever-pitch. At last, the whole figure of Ravana emerges, fighting with the curtain and then throwing it aside, accompanied by earth-shaking drumming, blood-curdling shrieks and the ominous sound of the conch. We know beyond doubt and against reason that this is Ravana incarnate in a human body (see p. 63). (This interlude with a curtain is known in *Kathakali* as *Tiranōkku* (literally "curtain look") and has special versions to suit different characters and situations.)

Afterwards we discover the main reason for the metamorphosis. The dancer-actor in question has studied *Kathakali* for 20 years, and has studied the character of Ravana until he knows *and feels* it inside out. Whilst the expert applies his make-up (the latter having served an apprenticeship of at least four years), which takes four hours, the actor sleeps and meditates on all he knows of Ravana. When he

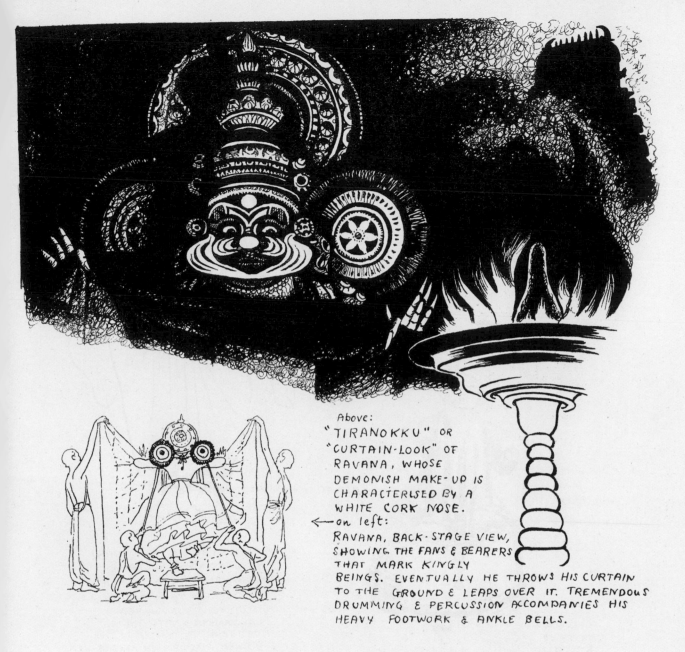

Above:
"TIRANOKKU" OR
"CURTAIN-LOOK" OF
RAVANA, WHOSE
DEMONISH MAKE-UP IS
CHARACTERISED BY A
WHITE CORK NOSE.
←on left:
RAVANA, BACK-STAGE VIEW,
SHOWING THE FANS & BEARERS
THAT MARK KINGLY
BEINGS. EVENTUALLY HE THROWS HIS CURTAIN
TO THE GROUND & LEAPS OVER IT. TREMENDOUS
DRUMMING & PERCUSSION ACCOMPANIES HIS
HEAVY FOOTWORK & ANKLE BELLS.

awakes, he *is* Ravana. He looks like him and feels like him. On this example the whole system of *Kathakali* dance-drama is based.

PRACTICAL AND TECHNICAL NOTES

Having given the bare outlines of the evolution of *Kathakali* dance-drama and afforded a glimpse at a contemporary performance, we will become as practical as space permits.

The tremendous melodrama which is *Kathakali* is propelled by a basic training which is second to none in pure scope. On the physical side the dancer must have perfect control of his body and limbs, which is achieved after at least twelve years of study and regular, special massage given by the feet of the masseur to the

A TRIUMPH OF MAKE-UP: HANUMAN, THE MONKEY-KING. (NOTE THE ACTOR'S REAL EYES JUST VISIBLE IN THE MONKEY "CHEEKS!")

COSTUME & MAKE-UP FOR KRISHNA.

A MALE DANCER, AS ·MOHINI, THE DANCING SEDUCTRICE. (KATHAKALI DANCE-DRAMA IS CONSIDERED TOO EXACTING & UNSUITABLE FOR WOMEN PERFORMERS.) NOTE THE ARTIFICIAL BOSOM, ALSO THE MARKED SIMILARITY OF THE HEAD ORNAMENTS & VEIL TO THOSE OF A MUSLIM LADY.

dancer as he lies on the ground. In ancient times every boy from Malabar and sometimes girls too underwent massage and had a few lessons in dancing as a matter of course. A feature of the training is the deep bend of the knees, and the turned-in feet. Dexterous and powerful footwork and rhythm are indispensable.

On the expressive side, let us state at the outset that a blank face makes a career in *Kathakali* out of the question. The *Kathakali* technique of using the face is a pure marvel of accomplishment, and Kunju Kurup is the greatest and most respected master of all. He still takes part in dance-dramas to-day, a lesson to the Western ballet with its age-limit: he is Ram Gopal's teacher of *Kathakali:* he is the leading teacher and exponent and has trained thousands of pupils: but such is the world of Indian dancing that I never heard his name even mentioned by anyone save Ram Gopal.

Some of the ancient masters have such control of their facial muscles and expressions that they can laugh with one side of their faces and (literally) cry with the other.

Every *Kathakali* dancer must be a master of both *tandava*, the vigorous masculine style demanded by duels and passages of pure dance, and *lasya*, the more lyrical style, and it is pure enchantment to see them change from one style to the other. *Lasya* is divided into two categories: one suitable for men (for presenting love-scenes, displays of sympathy, senti-ment and so on) and the other suitable for women, and boys who take female roles. As mentioned elsewhere, women may study *Kathakali* but may not take part in pure dance-drama which is too vigorous and difficult for them. (See *Sari-Dance*, pp. 66–67.)

"LOTUS" CONTAINING MIRROR FOR THE ACTOR TO LOOK AT HIS MAKE-UP

RED WOOL OR COTTON JACKET

LAYERS OF COTTON SKIRTS (PERHAPS 24): RED BORDER ON TOP ONE

WHITE & RED COTTON "LOTUS" BLOOMS

Below:

RAM GOPAL SLEEPS WITH HIS HEAD ON A WOODEN REST WHILE A KATHAKALI EXPERT APPLIES A MAKE-UP WHICH MAY TAKE AS MUCH AS 4 HOURS, THE ACTOR WAKING TRANSFORMED IN APPEARANCE & DISPOSITION TO THE CHARACTER HE IS TO PORTRAY.

Right: The finished make-up: King Rugmangada.

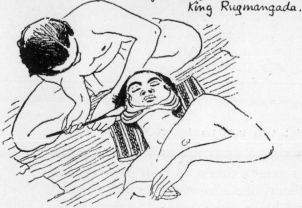

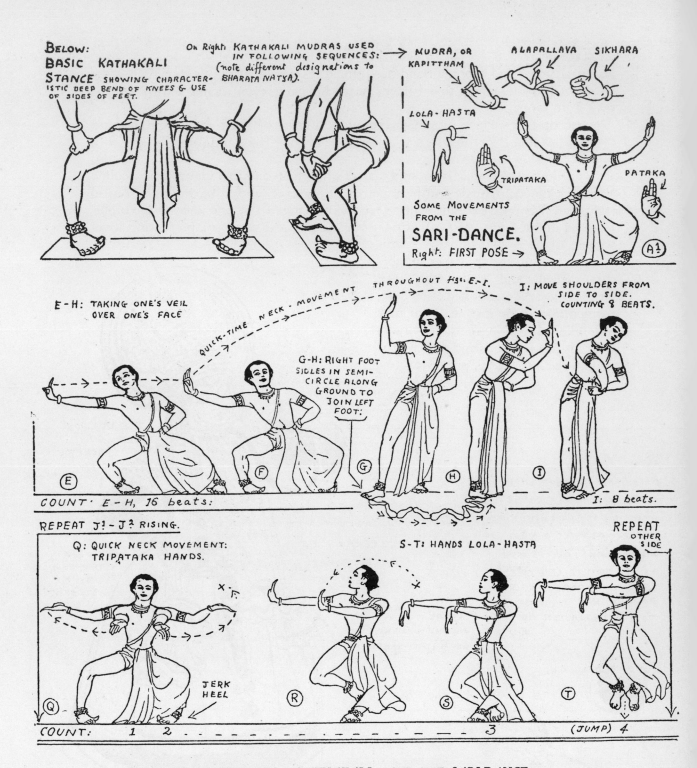

BASIC POSTURE OF *KATHAKALI*; AND THE *SARI-DANCE*

The highly conventional use of the sides of the feet has been developed by *Kathakali* dancers to save their soles from soreness after a 16 hour performance. It need not be adopted by more casual students of *Kathakali*, as it tends to affect natural stance (as it is intended to do) and looks unbecoming in other dance-

66

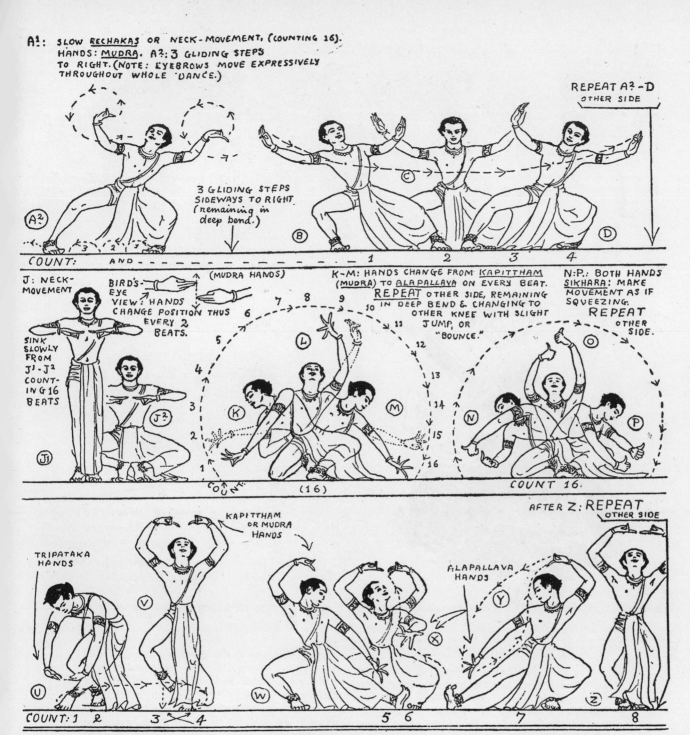

A¹: SLOW RECHAKAS OR NECK-MOVEMENT. (COUNTING 16).
HANDS: MUDRA. A²: 3 GLIDING STEPS
TO RIGHT. (NOTE: EYEBROWS MOVE EXPRESSIVELY
THROUGHOUT WHOLE DANCE.)

REPEAT A²-D
OTHER SIDE

3 GLIDING STEPS
SIDEWAYS TO RIGHT
(remaining in
deep bend.)

COUNT: AND - - - - - - - - - - - - - - 1   2   3   4

J: NECK-
MOVEMENT

BIRD'S
EYE
VIEW: HANDS
CHANGE POSITION THUS
EVERY 2
BEATS.

(MUDRA HANDS)

SINK
SLOWLY
FROM
J¹-J²
COUNTING 16
BEATS

K-M: HANDS CHANGE FROM KAPITTHAM
(MUDRA) TO ALAPALLAVA ON EVERY BEAT.
REPEAT OTHER SIDE, REMAINING
IN DEEP BEND & CHANGING TO
OTHER KNEE WITH SLIGHT
JUMP, OR
"BOUNCE."

N-P: BOTH HANDS
SIKHARA: MAKE
MOVEMENT AS IF
SQUEEZING.
REPEAT
OTHER
SIDE.

COUNT (16)   COUNT 16.

AFTER Z: REPEAT
OTHER SIDE

TRIPATAKA
HANDS

KAPITTHAM
OR MUDRA
HANDS

ALAPALLAVA
HANDS

COUNT: 1   2   3   4   5   6   7   8

styles. Imagine delicate *Bharata Natya* with these turned-in feet and the bandy
legs which the *Kathakali* dancer must cultivate!

The *Sari-dance* has many diverse and beautiful movements, a few of which are
sketched above, some of them based on an idea and some purely decorative. This
dance may be learned by women; is studied by men who must also have a complete
command of the *lasya* aspect of *Kathakali*, and by boys who dance female rôles in
all-night ballets.

REPEAT
OTHER
SIDE

KALASAMS
Example no. I.

HANDS:
ALAPALLAVA & MUDRA

F 4

COUNT: & 4 3 2 1 ← 3 2 1

KALASAM
Example no. II.
(A HUNTER.)

IMAGINARY STAGE

FACE
THIS
WAY

AUDIENCE

ABOVE: CHOREOGRAPHY
OF KALASAM no. I.
(Sequence A – F repeated
twice facing 4 different
directions.)

KATHAKALI KALASAMS

The word *Kalāsam* is probably derived from the Arabic term *Xalasa* meaning conclusion, especially in music. In *Kathakali* a *kalāsam* indicates a passage of vigorous dance, pure *tandava*, performed at the end of sung verses. The sketches above can give but little idea of the speed, agility and masculine vigour with which the various *kalāsams* can be performed. Such steps are an excellent illustration of *tandava* and only suitable for men. A suggestion of the choreography gives an impression of the virility of the dance performed in the flickering oil lamplight at speed.

In all the Indian dance-styles it is the choreo-graphy which is in the greatest danger of disappearing, owing to the superficial study accorded to the techniques as learned in a city classroom. *Kathakali* choreography is arranged for courtyard performances, *Kathak* choreography for palace court dancing with the audience all round the performer, *Bharata Natya* for gliding up and down long, mysterious temple chambers, and *Manipuri* often in a circular fashion like folk-dances and performed against a rustic background. Although these classical choreographic principles must sometimes be rearranged for the theatre, they must be borne in mind always, or the character of the individual style is lost.

PLATE IX

When embodied in Ram Gopal, every dance, no matter what the style, becomes understandable to us, the audience. But when through his own creations he speaks the very language of the immortal soul, the style he uses is that lyrical, profound and adaptable medium—basic *Kathakali*.

The Dance of the Setting Sun is a masterpiece with the same quality of "understandableness" as Pavlova's *Dying Swan*. When the last pink ray has vanished, and the sad flute ceases, there is always dead silence in the auditorium, followed by a storm of appreciation, the audience knows that it has seen a great creative work of art.

PLATE X

Above: LAUGHTER OF THE GODS. A photograph taken at the opening of the Indian Section of the Victoria and Albert Museum.

Left: DANCE OF THE HUNTER. The mood of fear . . . the Hunter espies an elephant. Ram Gopal learned this dance from Kunju Kurup when he was a young boy.

A FANTASY ON EXPRESSIVE DANCING: THE NINE MOODS OR *RASAS*

The robust and penetrating expressions of the *Kathakali* dance with their surprising subtlety, the delicate, religious seductiveness of the *Bharata Natya* invocational style, and the highly elegant and refined art of the expressive dancer of *Kathak* should all be performed in accordance with the "Nine Moods" as set down in Bharata's *Natya Sastras*. As allusions to these moods or sentiments are usually confined to photographs of the face, which give rise to the impression that they only concern the features, I have taken the liberty of underlining that all *situations* in Indian dancing should also be governed by these *rasas*, with the face, of course, as the principal indicator of the emotion involved. But in the mood of Fear, for example, the whole body and every movement should register terror, as well as the features.

On left: A-B: Example of BHARATA NATYA (COMBINED HAND) MUDRA, SYMBOLISING A PEACOCK:
A: PEACOCK WITH TAIL CLOSED:
B: PEACOCK WITH TAIL DISPLAYED.

FINGERS FLUTTER

1 & 2:) HAMSASYAM
4 & 5:) HANDS:

1-6: EXAMPLES OF KATHAKALI MUDRAS, EXPRESSIONS & MOVEMENTS SYMBOLISING A PEACOCK DANCING.

6: KATAKAMUKHA HANDS

MUDRAS.

MUDRAS, OR THE ANCIENT GESTURE-LANGUAGE OF THE INDIAN DANCE

It will have been noticed by now that there are confusing differences between the names of *Kathakali* and *Bharata Natya mudras*. In *Kathakali* alone, in the course of compiling this book I have been told four or five different names for one *mudra* by as many teachers on separate occasions, and feeling on the matter seems to run rather high. Consulting books only increases the confusion. So instead of trying to set down all these alternative names, I have used the ones I have found to be most frequently employed in each case and only noticed the genuine

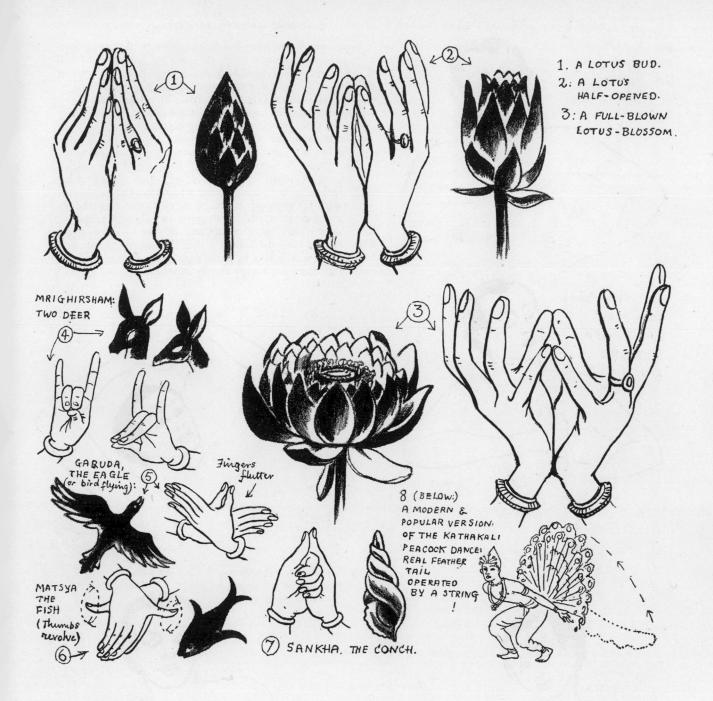

1. A LOTUS BUD.
2. A LOTUS HALF-OPENED.
3. A FULL-BLOWN LOTUS-BLOSSOM.

MRIGHIRSHAM: TWO DEER

GARUDA, THE EAGLE (or bird flying):

Fingers flutter

MATSYA THE FISH (Thumbs revolve)

⑦ SANKHA. THE CONCH.

8 (BELOW:) A MODERN & POPULAR VERSION OF THE KATHAKALI PEACOCK DANCE: REAL FEATHER TAIL OPERATED BY A STRING!

contradictions, *e.g.*, the reversed interpretations of the *pataka* and *tripataka mudras* in *Bharata Natya* and *Kathakali*. (See pp. 45 and 66.)

Fortunately where the *mudra* merely represents an object or an animal or bird, the confusion does not arise, and where possible I have used simply the name of the object as the name of the *mudra* in question.

Ram Gopal supplied the above information, along with most of the other material in this book, and the sketch of the lotus-*mudra* in particular reveals the unusual appearance of his hands in action.

71

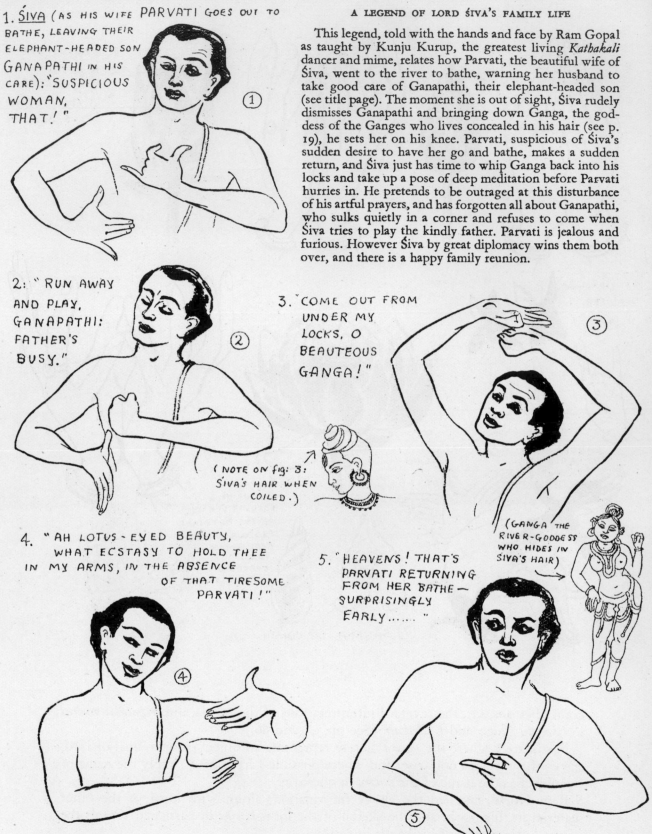

1. ŚIVA (AS HIS WIFE PARVATI GOES OUT TO BATHE, LEAVING THEIR ELEPHANT-HEADED SON GANAPATHI IN HIS CARE): "SUSPICIOUS WOMAN, THAT!"

This legend, told with the hands and face by Ram Gopal as taught by Kunju Kurup, the greatest living *Kathakali* dancer and mime, relates how Parvati, the beautiful wife of Śiva, went to the river to bathe, warning her husband to take good care of Ganapathi, their elephant-headed son (see title page). The moment she is out of sight, Śiva rudely dismisses Ganapathi and bringing down Ganga, the goddess of the Ganges who lives concealed in his hair (see p. 19), he sets her on his knee. Parvati, suspicious of Śiva's sudden desire to have her go and bathe, makes a sudden return, and Śiva just has time to whip Ganga back into his locks and take up a pose of deep meditation before Parvati hurries in. He pretends to be outraged at this disturbance of his artful prayers, and has forgotten all about Ganapathi, who sulks quietly in a corner and refuses to come when Śiva tries to play the kindly father. Parvati is jealous and furious. However Śiva by great diplomacy wins them both over, and there is a happy family reunion.

2: "RUN AWAY AND PLAY, GANAPATHI: FATHER'S BUSY."

3. "COME OUT FROM UNDER MY LOCKS, O BEAUTEOUS GANGA!"

(NOTE ON fig. 3: ŚIVA'S HAIR WHEN COILED.)

4. "AH LOTUS-EYED BEAUTY, WHAT ECSTASY TO HOLD THEE IN MY ARMS, IN THE ABSENCE OF THAT TIRESOME PARVATI!"

5. "HEAVENS! THAT'S PARVATI RETURNING FROM HER BATHE—SURPRISINGLY EARLY......"

(GANGA THE RIVER-GODDESS WHO HIDES IN ŚIVA'S HAIR)

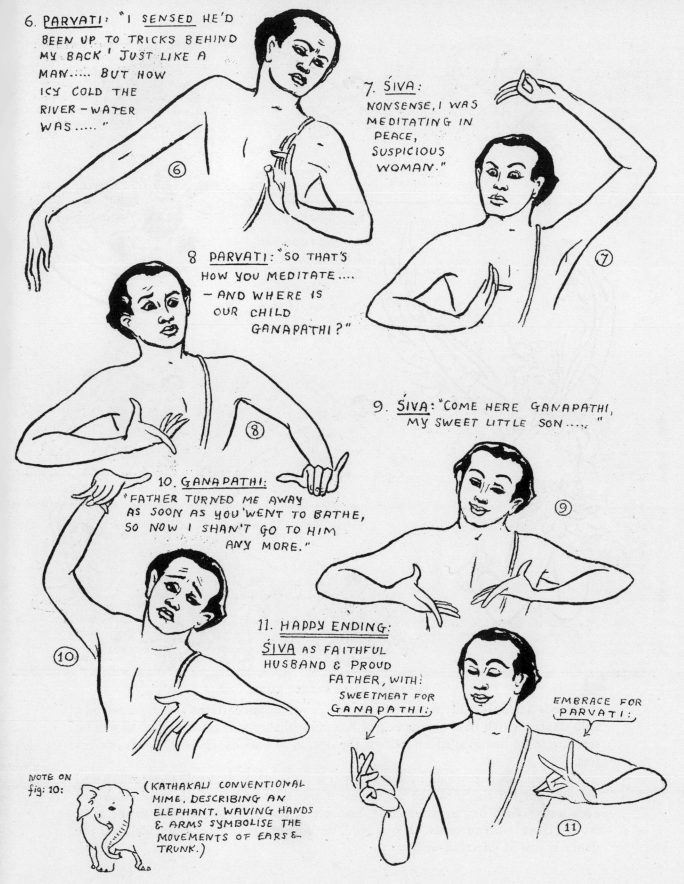

6. PARVATI: "I SENSED HE'D BEEN UP TO TRICKS BEHIND MY BACK! JUST LIKE A MAN..... BUT HOW ICY COLD THE RIVER-WATER WAS....."

7. ŚIVA: NONSENSE, I WAS MEDITATING IN PEACE, SUSPICIOUS WOMAN."

8 PARVATI: "SO THAT'S HOW YOU MEDITATE.... — AND WHERE IS OUR CHILD GANAPATHI?"

9. ŚIVA: "COME HERE GANAPATHI, MY SWEET LITTLE SON....."

10. GANAPATHI: "FATHER TURNED ME AWAY AS SOON AS YOU WENT TO BATHE, SO NOW I SHAN'T GO TO HIM ANY MORE."

11. HAPPY ENDING: ŚIVA AS FAITHFUL HUSBAND & PROUD FATHER, WITH: SWEETMEAT FOR GANAPATHI:

EMBRACE FOR PARVATI:

NOTE ON fig: 10: (KATHAKALI CONVENTIONAL MIME, DESCRIBING AN ELEPHANT. WAVING HANDS & ARMS SYMBOLISE THE MOVEMENTS OF EARS & TRUNK.)

73

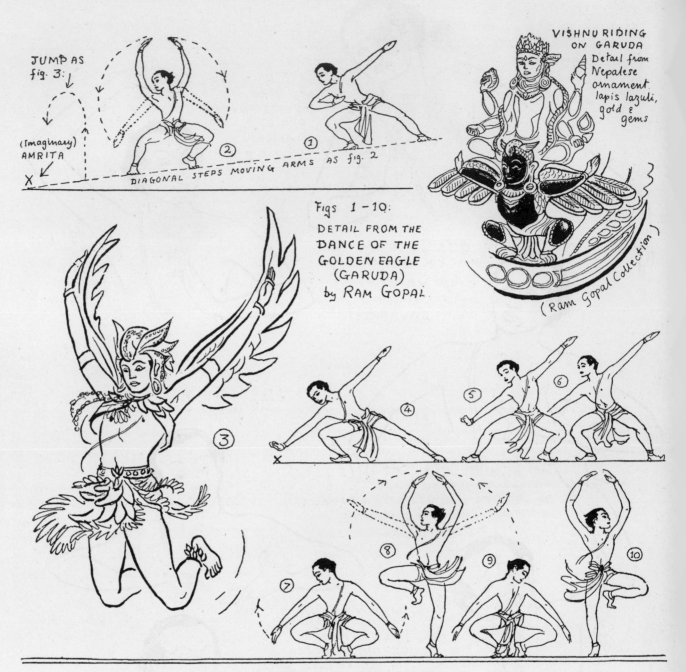

JUMP AS
fig. 3:

(Imaginary)
AMRITA

DIAGONAL STEPS MOVING ARMS AS fig. 2

VISHNU RIDING
ON GARUDA
Detail from
Nepalese
ornament
lapis lazuli,
gold &
gems

(Ram Gopal Collection)

Figs 1 – 10:
DETAIL FROM THE
DANCE OF THE
GOLDEN EAGLE
(GARUDA)
by RAM GOPAL

GARUDA, THE GOLDEN EAGLE

Here is a detail bodily removed from a *Kathakali* dance-drama and arranged as a solo-dance, which has become one of Ram Gopal's most famous items. As will be seen, here he has availed himself of the option not to dance on the sides of his feet.

The dance as performed by Ram Gopal is not only remarkable for its dash and vigour, but for the bird-like subtleties of the movements of his head, neck and eyes with which he has invested it, and which result, as is too seldom the case, from a close study of birds. Of real gold, the costume is an "eye-snatcher", but the dance is just as effective without it.

PLATE XI

Four studies of Ram Gopal as GARUDA,
THE GOLDEN EAGLE.

PLATE XII

Above: Ram Gopal surveys North India from a Moghul palace window. *Left:* Ram Gopal in the traditional Kathak costume (Denis de Marney).

Kumudini, talented *Kathak* dancer, impersonates the mischievous Blue God, Krishna.

A WATER-FÊTE AT NIGHT, WITH ILLUMINATED BARGE & KATHAK DANCING.
(From part of an unfinished miniature Rajput drawing, early 18th century.)

CHAPTER V

KATHAK

The *Kathak* dance of North India suffered until recently the same degradation as *Bharata Natya*, the ancient temple dance of the South Indian *bayadères* as described in a previous chapter, and for the same reasons. It deteriorated into an erotic and vulgar Nautch-dance (see sketch on p. 79) and came under the direct line-of-fire of the "Anti-Nautchers"; like all the other dance-styles, no quarter was given to the genuine classical performers, for the Voice of Morality invariably tips out the baby with the bath-water, artistically speaking. Had it not been for a certain art-loving Maharajah who maintained the best teachers and dancers at a regular salary at his own palace throughout the recent "dark ages" of Indian dancing, and so conserved the traditions of the art, it is hard to tell what would have happened to the present much-respected genuine *Kathak* school of dancing, which has preserved the original dynamic style, without which *Kathak* dancing is little more than a sort of voluptuous solo-perambulation punctuated by aimless spinning.

During their rule, which lasted about from the 14th to the 17th centuries, the Moghuls introduced into India their own style of court dance, an excessively elegant and refined art which had, however, no religious or spiritual significance whatever. The Moghul emperors as a majority encouraged all the arts at their courts, and the consequent employment of Hindu craftsmen and artists had the usual result—the Indians enriched everything they touched with their vitality and astonishing natural taste. The lacy, ivory elegance of the Persian palaces never equalled the dignity of the Taj Mahal, executed as it was by Hindu crafts-men; the early, purely Persian-style moghul miniature paintings, however exquisite, never blossomed out into the vigour, warmth and loving nature-study for which the later paintings are remarkable until the Hindu artists adopted (or rather, appropriated) the style, mingling it with their own indigenous art and producing such masterpieces that first-quality miniatures from, for example, Rajputana and the Kangra Valley, must now be placed on a level with the very greatest examples of decorative art and painting.

The Kathak dance developed in very much the same way. Starting as an elegant

75

and highly cultivated but purely decorative art, from its mingling with Hindu styles and convictions it gained a strong predominance of Hindu mythology; and like the paintings, which to begin with showed purely decorative subjects—conventional arrangements of hunting-scenes, and court-scenes which were gradually supplanted by the Indian way of looking at things with their colour, candour and observation, giving way to allegorical subjects which paved the way for out-and-out mythological paintings where the gods triumphantly dominated everything: even so the dance became gradually intermingled with Hindu thought and mythology and *Kathak* dancing may now be said, with certain reservations, to be practically the sole preserve of Radha, the shy sloe-eyed milk-maid and Sri Krishna, her mischievous boy-god suitor. Their amorous exchanges symbolise love of the Divine through the medium of music, dancing and singing (see *Ras Leela*, p. 22) in just the same way as ancient *Bharata Natya*.

It should be mentioned that the transition from decorative to religious art wasn't all fun for the Hindus, who were variously persecuted by their Moghul overlords for showing their forbidden beliefs. For a long time the painters of Krishna didn't survive to enjoy the admiration of their friends unless they hid those particular paintings, whilst the dancers judiciously took to their heels if they heard in time that some Moghul spy had carried a report of a Krishna *tukra* to official circles. Later, when the delights of persecution had palled the Moghuls took to public mockery of the Hindu *Kathak* dancers' insistence on religious interpolations in their technique; but finally, they gave it up in despair, and thus the Hindus patiently absorbed yet another foreign culture and made it their own.

In *Bharata Natya* the traditional postures, movements, ballets and orchestras are mostly recorded by the South Indian sculptures, bronzes and reliefs, with an occasional fading frescoe here and there; the preponderance of sculptures is probably due to the fact that it is easier for a vandal, or for a devout Mahommedan swiping merrily in the name of Allah, to destroy paintings than a colossal carved block of stone, whose missing noses and broken limbs bear testimony to the ferocity of centuries of religious onslaughts on art. But the records of *Kathak* dancing and its development are almost entirely represented by miniature paintings which supply with that microscopic detail which seldom if ever seems to destroy the effectiveness of the painting as a whole, the minutest information regarding costumes, jewellery, movement, environment, chapter and verse.

Radha and Krishna steal away together, lovers against the velvet dark blue of the night. Krishna, finding that an insulted King of the Gods, Indra, is sousing the earth with torrential rain, balances a mountain on the little finger of his left hand and invites the milkmaids and cows to take shelter underneath. He catches those same milkmaids swimming in the river and climbs a tree with all their clothes, causing much consternation in the water. On the festival of *Holi*, he squirts Radha with coloured water as she leans from her balcony: she replies by emptying coloured powder on the head of her lord, mourning her ruined *sari*. Siva, Parvati, and Ganesha picnic, misunderstand one another and make amends again. Gentle-eyed cows adorned with bells and necklaces listen enthralled to the melodies played on his flute by Krishna, the divine cowherd; delicately painted birds listen in blossoming trees, and Radha sets down her pot of whey, being careful not to step on the assembly of squirrels and mice who are also attending this celestial obligato.

A world of mixed and colourful enchantment; but to-day the *Kathak* dancer is rare who can make us smell those flowers, sense the soft fur of the fauns and evoke the gentle mystery of those starlit romances, where the miniaturist has painted with such sympathy two lovers planning an elopement.

From whence sprang the imposition imposed by many, that *Kathak* dancers may not make use of the ancient Hindu *mudras* and mime, that gesture-language of the classical *Sastras* which is the fount of all Indian dance, to help give life to their dances? To conserve the technique alone from the days of the Moghul court-dances is like exhibiting a painter's brushes and palette and locking his paintings in the attic.

The *Kathak* dance-style as it may be learned to-day was founded by the master Maharaj Binda Din, whose portrait is to be found in the leading dance academies, an object of much respect. He codified and wrote down all that was best in the dance of his day; before he did this, the dance lived only in the heads of performers and teachers, a precarious condition for an art form of such transience.

Binda Din must have been a fabulously gifted performer of *Kathak* dancing in all its aspects, and a man of great patience and learning to record what he knew in such detail. In *Kathak* dancing, *tandava* describes this fiery technique as it is performed by a dancer who stands and moves about; and *lasya* is the aspect in which the dancer kneels, or remains immobile the whole time except for the *gât* as described later on, and tells stories with his expressive powers only, with his face and hands, and it is astonishing what enchantment such a "dancer" can weave. To-day I believe the dancer who excels in both these aspects, the *tandava* and the *lasya*, is unknown; performers invariably specialise in either *tandava* or *lasya*, and one who can act cannot perform brilliant dance-sequences, and the other way about. Binda Din left behind him a complete account of suitable instructions for the gesture-stories, and a wonderful school of pure dance technique covering the *tandava* aspect of the art, a vigorous, brilliant and powerful style which can be performed with relative ease to a recurrent beat of 8, known as *trital*, or developed until one sequence can embrace over 100 beats at a stretch of crossed, interwoven rhythms which need a brain which combines a memory like an elephant, a capacity for working out algebraic problems with sharp slaps of the feet, and a clocklike sense of basic time. (An appreciative audience needs the same qualities!)

The most celebrated propounder of this school to-day is Jailal,* who teaches the pure technique in both its aspects. (He is held by his students in the same esteem as Enrico Cecchetti was held by his pupils of the ballet.) His is the *classe-de-perfection*, his pupils few and chosen with care. And, like the Western ballet, and most other dance-forms, *Kathak* can be divided into two main sections: the pure and classical style, which takes much study, and the softened-up, popular, fashion-able and easy-to-master version.

This voluptuous style is marked by a number of publicity-tricks, and specialises

* Just before going to press, I learn with deep regret that Jailal died suddenly in Calcutta. His chief pupil, Radhelal Misra, is now with Ram Gopal as *Kathak* teacher.

in stunts to impress the credulous. For example, red sand is sprinkled on the floor and dancers draw outlines of simple objects with their feet in the course of a gliding-step closely resembling the *pas-de-bourrée* of the ballet dancer, the resulting design being afterwards displayed with great bravura. Dancers claim they can perform this gliding step on gauze without wrinkling it and a large reward is offered to anyone who can espy a crease, and so forth. (Publicity-loving *yogis* do tricks in the same spirit, to attract attention, and are much despised on this account by genuine *yogis*.) The consequence of all this is a large and prosperous school of gracefully ineffectual *Kathak* dancers who can only perform to a time of 8 beats to a bar. And anyway, a modern *Kathak* dancer can really do whatever he likes in a display of dancing, and if anyone questions his or her authenticity the over-worked reply is invariably "but that is the style *I* learned."

The serious student of classical *Kathak* dancing won't have nearly so much fun and very hard work indeed, but his rewards are of course infinitely greater. In *his* school, your teacher is apt to put bricks around your feet and if you move off the spot in your *chukras* (or whipping brilliant turns) bruised toes will teach you a memorable lesson.

Those *chukras* are the trademark of *Kathak* dancing, the most sensational and easily remembered feature. Some remarkable girl-dancers turn so fast that you can't see them but can clearly hear their black plait of hair whistling through the air like a whip. Others have been known to crack concrete floors with their foot-work: and these aren't publicity stunts, but accessories after the fact of their terrific dance-style.

The footwork or *tatkar* of *Kathak* dancing should be especially noticed as it could be studied with benefit by students of any one of the Indian classical dance-styles, and often is. Even the basic step, starting slowly and gaining speed like a number of gears, is an exercise in itself, as however fast the feet fly, the separate beats must be clearly discernible and no blurring can be countenanced.

Here is a summary of the main terms in Kathak dancing, and their meanings and functions in the classroom:

1. *TATKAR*. As described above, this term embraces the powerful foot-work in the form of an exercise, including the complicated cross-rhythms.

2. *THÁT*. A kind of opening gambit, an example of which can be found at the top of p. 81, featuring the characteristic use of the head with slight, crisp changes of direction. This is usually followed by a stylised "walk", an example of which can be seen at the foot of the same page.

3. *GÁT*. A short decorative or descriptive passage performed in rather a lyrical manner to a gentle rhythm. Classified to-day as *lasya*.

4. *TORAH*. The first *torah* to be performed in a *Kathak* class should be the "*salami*" (see top of p. 82) which is a greeting to the audience or master, and takes the place of the *Bharata Natya* "*namaskaram*" (see p. 51), and is also com-parable to the traditional curtesy performed to the teacher at the conclusion of a Western dancing-class. Substantially, a *torah* is a fast and brilliant dance-sequence which, however, includes *sangit*, or dramatic content in addition to dance-technique: *e.g.*, "*salami*" contains a salute.

5. *TUKRA*. A dance-sequence, pure, brilliant and fast, showing technique alone.

Kathak performed as a Nautch Dance. (From a lithograph dated 1858.)
Ram Gopal collection.

Here, there is no place to go into the highly specialised question of *Kathak* rhythms, but it will give the reader an idea of the general set-up to know that as far as the ordinary dance-company is concerned, a much simplified and usually slightly corrupt version of *Kathak* is employed as a vehicle for unimportant ballet-themes, using the easy *trital*, composed of 4 groups of 4 beats, or two of 8 beats, adding up to 16 and corresponding to the simplest Western basic time. The *Kathak* dance specialist in *tandava* may develop dances based on any basic time, great or small, odd or even, up to over a hundred beats at a time, carrying the basic beat in his or her head, dancing cross-times and counterpoint and always ending on *sum*, or one beat after the prescribed number has been finished. The drummer maintains staccato descriptive chant and rhythm on the double-drums, *tabla* and *baya*, or on the more classical *mahamrdang*, and the melody is played on an instrument such as the *sarangi* (see instruments on pp. **28–29**). A local audience knows the number of beats because of the melody, and they applaud when dancer,

79

drummer and instrumentalist all reach a climax simultaneously on the beat, *sum*.

So a finished *Kathak* technician can choose an awkward time, such as groups of 9, 10 or 11 beats, and perform a whole dance in accordance with it, including *thât*, *gât*, and all the rest of it, but it is certainly not worth taking all that trouble unless the audience can appreciate such efforts; and the only audience capable of understanding such a complicated affair would have to be composed of *Kathak* teachers, pupils, professors, etc. Nevertheless, in comparatively simple *tal*, or timing, there is plenty of scope for the accomplished *Kathak* dancer to delight the eye and capture the senses in a way that is more easily understood, and—let us admit—nearer to that universality which should be the goal of the real artist.

All the same, at the present time the average North Indian will refer to *Kathakali*, the South Indian dance-drama of Malabar, as a crude devil-dance, solemnly maintaining that contamination will result from witnessing such heavy vulgarity; and the South Indians are moved to giggles and boredom by *Kathak*, reciting the *Natya Sastras* and the penalties for watching inferior dancers. Happily, in the West both arts are assured of a warm welcome, and understanding is growing with what rapidity it may.

In conclusion, a word on costume: as worn to-day, *Kathak* costumes may be classified as follows: (i) Those generally worn—which are often neither becoming, comfortable, nor in accordance with tradition; (ii) Those which have been adjusted to conform to public taste as guided by film-promoters (concerning which the less said the better), and those few which are designed in accordance with the

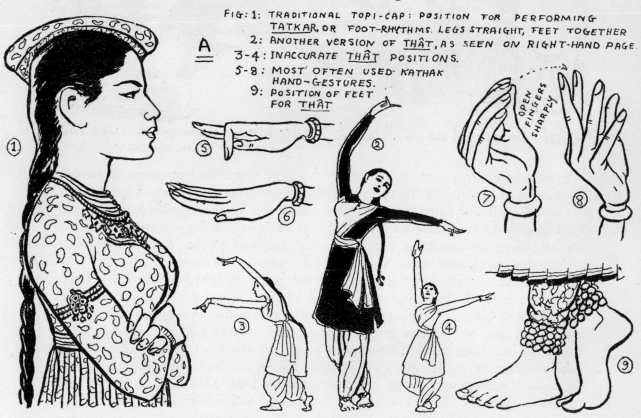

FIG: 1: TRADITIONAL TOPI-CAP: POSITION FOR PERFORMING
TATKAR, OR FOOT-RHYTHMS. LEGS STRAIGHT, FEET TOGETHER
A   2: ANOTHER VERSION OF THÂT, AS SEEN ON RIGHT-HAND PAGE.
—   3-4: INACCURATE THÂT POSITIONS.
      5-8: MOST OFTEN USED KATHAK
           HAND-GESTURES.
      9: POSITION OF FEET
         FOR THÂT

OPEN FINGERS SHARPLY

innumerable and magnificent records provided by the Moghul, Rajput, Kangra and other styles of miniature paintings which cover the last 3–4 centuries of North Indian dance and costume development. A study of these paintings will reveal that the artists appreciated to the full that the *Kathak* dance, with its whirling and spinning, should be accentuated by a *ghagara*,* or immensely full skirt, such as many North Indian women wear to this day; they refrained from painting

1 - 5. ONE OF THE MANY VERSIONS OF <u>THÂT</u> AS A PRELIMINARY TO A DANCE.

(HEAD TURNS SHARPLY)

4ᴬ - 5ᴬ: GIRL-DANCER HOLDS HER HANDS SLIGHTLY PARTED (MANS ARE ONE UPON THE OTHER.)

B

① ② ③ ④ ⑤ 4ᴬ 5ᴬ

COUNT: AND 1 2 3 .... 4.

C 1. PRINCIPAL KATHAK DANCE-POSITION; <u>THÂT</u>.

2 - 5: CHARACTERISTIC GLIDING KATHAK "WALK".

NECK MOVEMENT TWICE

NECK MOVEMENT TWICE

① SLIDE R. FOOT FORWARD ② ③ LIFT L. HEEL & ROCK SLIGHTLY ④ ⑤

"THÂT" COUNT: AND 1, 2: AND 1, 2:

* Ghagara, see p. 91

A SALĀMI: TORAH
BASED ON TRITAL: (8 beats.)

1-2: Two BIG STRIDES FORWARD

HEAD MOVEMENT

REPEAT 5, 6, 7

FEET:	R	L		RLRL	LRLR	R		L	—	(RL—)	R		L	—
TIME:	1			2	3		4			5 (6,7)		8			9 ("SŪM").

(figures numbered 1 2 3 4 5 6 →7 8 9 10)

dancers attired in *saris*, a dancer spinning in a *sari* is a clumsy sight. But many masters believe the *sari* to be the traditional dress for *Kathak* dancing. As to the men: look at the traditional Rajput court dress on p. 91, and then at the same person dancing in white leggings, waistcoat and *topi*-cap on p. 83, and then compare this with the sketches at the base of this page The costume on p. 83. is accounted the best and most traditional to-day, although miniatures invariably show the full, pleated skirts for dancers, male and female, if one excepts Krishna's

B TUKRA BASED ON TRITAL: (8 BEATS, MATRAS or BARS.)
HANDS: see figs. 7-8 previous page

CLAP   CLAP   SHARP MOVEMENT

RHYTHM:	TA	THUNGA	TAKA	THUNGA	TIKADHET		TA THUNGA
FEET:	R	RL	RL	RL	R L R		R L R
TIME:	1	2		3			4

(figures numbered 1 2 3 4 5 6 7)

REPEAT SEQUENCE 11-12-13 3 TIMES

	TAKA	DIGADIGADIGADIGADIGADIGA	THAI	TA	TA	THAI
	L R	12 HEEL-BEATS ON GROUND	R	R	L	R (RLR:RLR)
	5	6		7		(8 9.)

(figures numbered 8 9 10 11 12 13)

82

yellow *dhoti* or trousers; but even the *dhoti* has more movement than those white, tight leggings.

The genuine *Kathak* dance, on which the sketches in this book are based and which retains all the latent brilliance of the original style, is a matchless technique; but it needs rejuvenation for stage-presentation and a return to classical principles of costume and presentation, as do almost all the other traditional Indian dance styles. It is necessary to restore to these dances the charm some of them have undoubtedly lost through antiquity; the technical vitality is there, the records of costumes and ornaments, the requisite mythological data, but the majority of the dancers seem unable to put everything together and therefore much of the original splendour is lacking. Of course, *Kathak* dancing on an illuminated barge (see p. 75) is one thing: the dry and uninspiring atmosphere of the modern concert-hall, where the same steps and movements are apt to look dreadfully dull, is quite another. Without losing this wonderful and vital dance-technique, a way must be found between modernisation, which is always dangerous, and over-academicism, which is dull; but re-vitalisation is imperative.

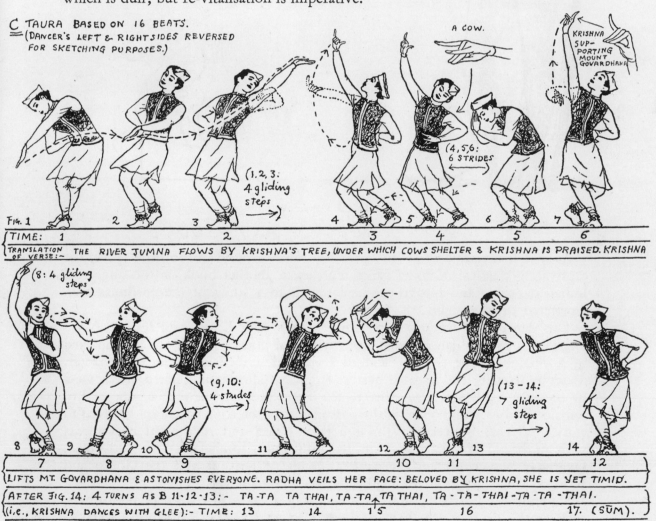

C TAURA BASED ON 16 BEATS.
(DANCER'S LEFT & RIGHT SIDES REVERSED FOR SKETCHING PURPOSES.)

A COW.

KRISHNA SUPPORTING MOUNT GOVARDHANA

(1, 2, 3: 4 gliding steps →)

(4, 5, 6: 6 STRIDES →)

FIG. 1   2   3   4   5   6   7

TIME: 1   2   3   4   5   6

TRANSLATION OF VERSE:— THE RIVER JUMNA FLOWS BY KRISHNA'S TREE, UNDER WHICH COWS SHELTER & KRISHNA IS PRAISED. KRISHNA

(8: 4 gliding steps →)

(9, 10: 4 strides →)

(13 - 14: 7 gliding steps →)

8   9   10   11   12   13   14

7   8   9   10   11   12

LIFTS MT. GOVARDHANA & ASTONISHES EVERYONE. RADHA VEILS HER FACE: BELOVED BY KRISHNA, SHE IS YET TIMID.
AFTER FIG. 14: 4 TURNS AS B 11·12·13:— TA-TA TA THAI, TA-TA TA THAI, TA-TA-THAI-TA-TA-THAI.
(i.e., KRISHNA DANCES WITH GLEE):— TIME: 13   14   15   16   17. (SŪM).

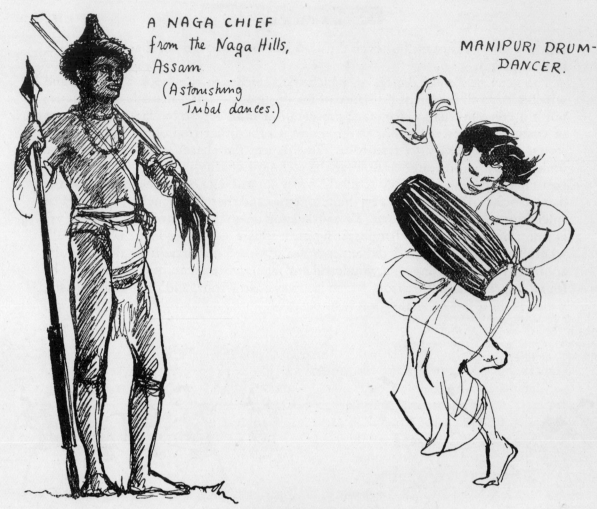

A NAGA CHIEF
from the Naga Hills,
Assam
(Astonishing
Tribal dances.)

MANIPURI DRUM-
DANCER.

CHAPTER VI

DANCES OF MANIPUR AND ASSAM

As it is inadvisable to try to cover too much ground in too little space, the captivating classical *Manipuri* dance must await another book on the subject of Indian dancing; and I have confined myself to a study of the costumes seen illustrated on the right.

This dance style has much in common with both *Kathak* and *Bharata Natya* techniques, as it is danced mostly in rhythmical phrases which are accompanied by a version of the *bols* or "winged words" described in a previous chapter. *Manipuri* dancing has its own gesture-language, almost obliterated from view by the excessively soft grace with which it is expressed; the face is supposed to remain absolutely immobile, as the movements of the dance itself are believed to convey all that is necessary through their lyrical and rhythmical movements without the aid of facial expression. Beautiful and leisurely ballets are performed, invariably woven around the gentle legends of Krishna and the Gopis, and accompanied by songs often sung by the dancers themselves.

Manipur also boasts vigorous dance-solos of great virility for male performers, such as the drum-dance sketched here; also wild but well-organised warrior-

84

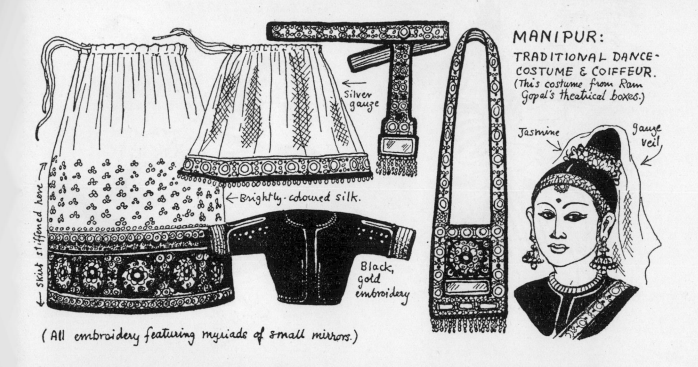

MANIPUR:
TRADITIONAL DANCE-
COSTUME & COIFFEUR.
(This costume from Ram
Gopal's theatrical boxes.)

Silver gauze

Jasmine

gauze veil

← Brightly-coloured silk.

← Skirt stiffened here

Black, gold embroidery

(All embroidery featuring myriads of small mirrors.)

dances. Further North in the Naga hills, warriors perform less organised and even wilder dances. Incredible Tantric dances and the like are still performed by old women, and surprising group-dances closely resembling the American square-dance, with a leader who announces each successive step, are performed in costumes which the average critic would certainly denounce as Spanish, but which date back further than one would care to guess.

KRISHNA AND THE GOPIS: the favourite subject for a Manipuri ballet. (Ram Gopal dances in the open air.)

85

FUR HATS in ↙ SOUTH INDIA! (Part of an invocational Folk-Dance.)

DAMARU (for calling ← SIVA)

STICK (for beating The Devil.)

Ram Gopal joins in a Folk Dance in MARWAR, (North India.)

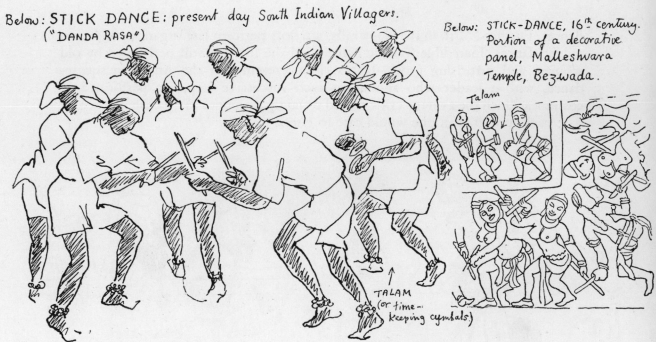

Below: STICK DANCE: present day South Indian Villagers. ("DANDA RASA")

Below: STICK-DANCE, 16th century. Portion of a decorative panel, Malleshwara Temple, Bezwada.

Talam

TALAM (or time-keeping cymbals)

CHAPTER VII
A PATCHWORK OF INDIAN FOLK-DANCES

Chosen at random from my sketchbooks these colourful dances show villagers at play. The stick-dance, the staff-dance and many others crop up all over the world. Sowing and reaping corn are also international occupations and tend to be expressed in the same way, but some folk-dances based on Indian mythology are India's own. Here, the costumes showing cotton shorts and shirts are Western, but it is their capacity to absorb and digest alien influences which make folk-dances what they are. If you treat them with classical solemnity their gaiety and spontaneity leaves them.

A STAFF-DANCE. (PERFORMED BY MYSORE VILLAGERS IN CELEBRATION OF THE DASARA FESTIVITIES.)

One of the many clever patterns made by the dancers. Above, they are revolving and performing a step just like the Cossack-dancers at the same time: with the brilliant colours, an indescribably gay effect.

12 MEN →

KHOMBA KANKARIA: A *puja*, or invocation to the god of the Neem-tree. Drawn at night in a valley near Aladeniya, Ceylon.

Dangerous job: this man must precede the dancers with a coconut filled with blazing oil. Frequently the dancers, etc., landed amongst the spectators.

CHAPTER VIII

DANCES OF CEYLON

Ceylon, supposed by some to be the original site of the Garden of Eden, has survived a number of complete foreign dominations, but despite this it has managed to conserve an ancient classical dance-style, although this is now in an extremely fragmentary condition.

That it survived at all is partly due to the fact that to stamp out a form of dancing which is one with religious practices is a well-nigh impossible task, and partly to a version of the "artist-caste" system similar to that which has preserved the art of *Kathakali* in Malabar. In Ceylon whole villages produce dancers and drummers, just as some villages produce a family of master-weavers or potters; but the depressingly violent jealousy between many of the different families has all but undone the excellence of the caste-system, and the apparent disregard of the Sinhalese for the artistic value of their dances (dancers and drummers being considered unsuitable to enter the houses of the élite) has done nothing to help the situation.

Perhaps the best known dancer and teacher of the traditional Kandyan dance is Gunaya; the drawings above and on page 89 show Nittawela Mulyaddessalagadera Ukkuwa, also a great exponent, teacher and preserver of Kandyan dancing, as were his ancestors before him. He is sketched in full Kandyan costume performing the dance of the mythological elephant for Ram Gopal, and at the top of this page taking the lead in *Khomba Kankaria*, a great religious *puja* to the god of the neem-tree; other sketches are from the *Pera-hera*, in this case the largest religious procession of all *pera-heras* which features the transportation of the Buddha's Tooth through the streets of Kandy.

PLATE XIII

Nittawela Mulyaddessalagadera Ukkuwa, a leading exponent of Kandyan dancing to-day.

Left: ANURA shows *Bera*, a Sinhalese drum-dance, to Western audiences.
Right: UKKUWA and two fellow-dancers performing a traditional dance in Kandy, Ceylon.

PLATE XIV. FROM THE ALBUM OF RAM GOPAL'S COMPANY.

Above: Londoners queue in the rain outside the Princes Theatre, London.
Left: Nijinsky takes tea with Ram Gopal at the Saville Theatre, London, 1948. *Daily Graphic photograph.*

Ram Gopal explains drumming to Pierino Gamba, the boy conductor, in Copenhagen.

Ram Gopal in Paris, in the Champs Elysées.

Part of traditional Indian dancing: Ram Gopal prays before a performance.

Snow! Kumudini sees her first snow-storm in Scandinavia.

Expectancy! the stage and orchestra await Ram Gopal.

Spring in Stockholm. The girls enjoy the park.

THE PERA-HERA, A RELIGIOUS PROCESSION IN KANDY Drawn by torchlight

CEREMONIAL DRUMMER-DANCER

UKKUWA at a special performance for Ram Gopal, describes a sacred elephant's trunk, using classical symbolism

Baby Elephant

PANTÉRU:
A traditional Sinhalese dance which takes its name from the instrument cleverly handled by the dancer.
(In this case, part of the Pera-hera procession.)

Another Khomba Kankaria dancer.

CHAPTER IX

COSTUMES OF INDIA

Too often the whole subject of Indian dress is treated in the West as a quaint survival from a past age, having no relation to the present day and to be treated with solemn and detached curiosity or blank incredulity. On the contrary the Indian master-weaver's unbelievable flair for making fabulous materials, the dyer's inexpressible inventions and designs, and the Indian person's talent for wearing the result, is a living inspiration not only to the artist but to every elegant woman in any part of the globe; and of course, to every dancer.

In this short account of Indian dress, Western readers will be particularly concerned with discovering some means whereby they can tell whether an Indian dancer's costumes are "fake", "westernised", or correct, so I would draw their attention to the following observations. The three faults most common in assessing Indian dance costumes are:—

(i) That Western critics are unaware of the endless variety and comprehensiveness of Indian dress. Anything which suggests to them Spain, Paris, Mexico or Russia is immediately denounced in chorus, when one may reflect that even in the unlikely event of the average critic having visited India, he would certainly have done so via a succession of Government Houses beginning and ending with some cosmopolitan port-town. But it should be born in mind that there is no dress or detail of a costume in the world which cannot be found in some sort in India, from frank, bare skin to a furry esquimau. For instance, in South India the ancient traditional *sari* still worn by peasants is often a many-coloured check material. If you wore one on the stage under the banner of India every critic would try to be the first to say you bought it in Scotland. What is particularly interesting is the fact that our Western "gypsies", who are of Indian origin (and who characteristically hold the general monopoly of fortune-telling in the West) will do almost anything to lay their hands on a piece of tartan, plaid or checked material in gay colours. But when an Indian costume really is Westernised, it can be felt instinctively, and Westernisation is more a matter of the way you wear things than what you wear. A *sari* can look just like a cheap evening-gown when worn with a profusion of brooches, as it is by some non-Indian residents of Bharat . . . and 6 yards of beautiful French silk in a clear and lovely colour can look like a first-class *sari* if worn by an Indian lady of taste. So hestitate before making rash statements *re* authenticity!

(ii) In the West there are a certain number of preconceived ideas concerning Indian costume which are occasionally played up by Indian dancers. One idea pertains to *danse orientale* in which India and the whole orient are lumped together, the costume for which can best be described as two saucepan lids, a postage-stamp and a tiara. The other fixed idea is that if the costumes are dowdy, then they *must* be authentic (poor, overworked word), which indicates a gloomy tendency to confuse the dust of a museum with the value of its contents. This misapprehension extends also to criticisms of dancing—"I didn't understand it, and it was terribly dull, but obviously real", to paraphrase a characteristic *critique*. So it should be born in mind too that if dances are advertised as Indian, and prove to be dull, then there is likely to be something wrong with the dancer and not, sir or madam, with you.

(iii) The average dancer of *Bharata Natya* and his or her teacher will tell you that the *devadasi's* costume on p. 37 is the authentic one for this ancient dance, and it is true that it is the one which is most often seen in India to-day. But the heavily overdressed appearance, bulky "apron" and pantaloons which conceal the dancer's lines do not appear before the Victorian era, and are diametrically opposed to the other sketch on the same page, the lines of which are classical.

THE CLASSICAL & TRADITIONAL COURT DRESS OF RAJPUTANA. NORTH INDIA:
(Ram Gopal wears his ancestral costume.)

Westernisation is not a taint which arrived on the first shipment of films from Hollywood, but long before. In *Bharata Natya* and many other dance styles a return to the main principles of classical outline is imperative, not in a pedantic,

A FEW DRAPERIES FROM THE SOUTH

archæological spirit but one of rejuvenation, in keeping with the contemporary Indian dance-renaissance.

In the course of sketching dance sequences from different parts of India,

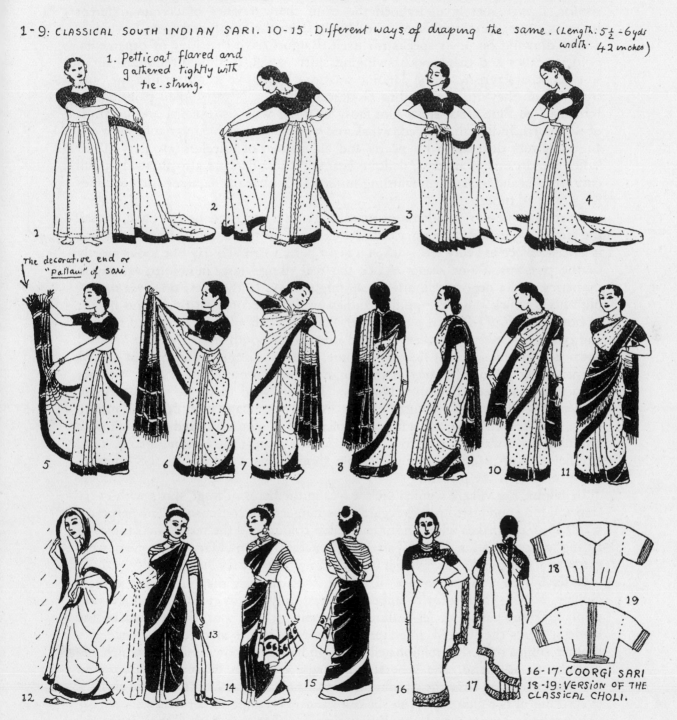

1-9: CLASSICAL SOUTH INDIAN SARI. 10-15 Different ways of draping the same. (Length: 5½-6yds width: 42 inches)

1. Petticoat flared and gathered tightly with tie-string.

The decorative end or "Pallau" of sari

16-17: COORGI SARI 18-19: VERSION OF THE CLASSICAL CHOLI.

MORE DRAPERIES FROM THE SOUTH

besides indicating as much as possible of the full-dress costumes, I also show the local costumes as worn by the dancers and students—although Indian dancers like Western ones tend to wear anything they fancy for dance-practice. In this section I have merely underlined the main characteristics of certain different styles of dress, an example from the North, from the South and from Ceylon.

The drawing on p. 91 speaks for itself. Rajputs have that love of ornaments, gold brocades and diaphanous swinging skirts which is almost feminine but is so often characteristic of the genuine warrior. They love to glitter like the Sun, from whom they are supposed to be descended. The North Indian paintings of Krishna, the Blue God, show him fairly bristling with ornaments, and portraits of the North Indian sharp-eyed, whiskered warrior-monarchs invariably show the august sitters dripping with pearls and all manner of priceless jewellery. Their ladies are dreams of modest, delicate beauty. Their dancers also dressed in full court regalia and to set them whirling in *saris* and other uncharacteristic costumes is a waste of time.

There are literally hundreds of ways of tying a *sari*, and here I have chosen the simplest method of tying a classical example, in the South Indian *sari* which is a masterpiece in every way—when it is properly worn. To-day one looks mostly to the peasants if one wants to see the real thing—taste in colour, artistry in draperies, and a deportment any queen might envy. In the West one sees mostly high-heels which cause the gliding Indian walk to become a slouch, and horror of horrors, a *choli* (classical blouse) with "built-up" shoulders and puffed sleeves, and only an occasional beauty. But the streets of a South Indian village or small town is a kaleidoscope of floating colours, figures as supple and upright as lily-stems. A dark-skinned beauty in an orange *sari* with a poison-pink *choli*. Another beauty in black edged with a blood-red border, gold earrings, silver tinkling anklets and a basket of pale green limes. A Mysore village with décor of mauve earth, grey-leaved trees, and a file of women clad in wine-coloured *saris* each with a shining brass water-pot, drifting like goddesses against the blinding green of the rice-fields, with a dusty, horned temple shouldering a thicket in the distance. Here the past is the present.

In Jaipur, the village women kick waves in the hems of huge skirts with every step and long and lustrous eyes regard the stranger with composure. The perpetual water shortage makes white an impracticable colour, and the result is costumes of flaring yellows and reds and patterned, emerald green. Marwari women wear skirts and veils, and a jewel like a miner's lamp on their foreheads.

India herself is a storehouse of magic, with colours that injure the eyes, a climate ranging from snow to unbearable heat, tiny deadly insects and huge kind elephants; and an ideal, all-healing philosophy which soothes the soul of the restless, pities the wicked, tolerates the ignorant, smiles at modern science as a mother smiles on a self-opinionated child. India has her own miracles which she disdains to advertise. She venerates her wise old men, whose sweetness and wisdom combined have the cleanliness of an English hayfield. And as she absorbs everything in her philosophy, so she can show everything in her dances.

Everybody cannot visit India. But anyone who has seen Ram Gopal dance has seen the very soul of India herself.

BIBLIOGRAPHY

Readers are recommended to the following books, being a selection of those consulted by the author, and borrowed from the library of Ram Gopal. They are all readily understandable.

EPICS, MYTHS AND LEGENDS OF INDIA, by P. Thomas (D. B. Taraporevala Sons & Co., Bombay).
An excellent, amusing and instructive pantechnicon of mythological India, its deities and beliefs, with copious illustrations and lively and humane text.

DANCE OF ŚIVA, by Ananda K. Coomaraswamy. THE MIRROR OF GESTURE, by Ananda K. Coomaraswamy and Duggiriala Gopalakrishnayya.
All books by the late Dr. Coomaraswamy are of interest to the student of Indian thought, as his only compromise with the West was his splendid and readable command of English.

IDEALS OF INDIAN ART, INDIAN SCULPTURE AND PAINTING, A HANDBOOK OF INDIAN ART, THE HIMALAYAS IN INDIAN ART, etc., by E. B. Havell. (John Murray, London.)
Mr. E. B. Havell's books are remarkable for their fearless defence of Indian art at a time when it was grossly misunderstood. The Western reader will find all his works highly informative, interesting and very readable.

BALI, by Miguel Covarrubias.
The only acknowledged authoritative book on Balinese dance-drama.

PERSONALITIES IN PRESENT-DAY MUSIC, by E. Krishna Iyer, B.A., B.L.
Mr. Iyer is the leading critic on the Indian temple-dance, and he was largely responsible for its revival. All his pamphlets and articles are full of first-hand information, and readers should secure whatever works they can by this notable author.

SOUTH INDIAN BRONZES, by O. C. Gangoly. (1915: Thacker, India: and Luzac, London.)
A rare volume, beautifully illustrated, and with many references to the *Silpasastras*—ancient texts dealing with art.

ATTAKATHA or KATHAKALI, by P. Krishnan Nayar.
The author discusses *Kathakali* with energy, authority and an unusual lack of bias. The introduction only is in English. A later book, by the same author, viz. KATHAKALI, THE MALABAR DANCE, is all in English.

KATHAKALI, THE SACRED DANCE DRAMA OF MALABAR, by K. Bharata Iyer. (Luzac, London.)
This author is perhaps the most well-known authority on Kathakali. The above volume is illustrated with splendid photographs.

THE ART AND ARCHITECTURE OF BIKANER STATE, by Hermann Goetz. (Bruno Cassirer, Oxford.)
Of especial interest as it deals with the development of one particular style, particularly of miniature-painting, in relation to its sister arts. Usually all schools of miniature-painting are lumped together.

THE HINDU TEMPLE, vols. I and II, by Stella Kramrisch, a rare work with many beautiful photographs by Raymond Burnier.

THE BRIDE'S BOOK OF BEAUTY, by Mulk Raj Anand and Krishna Hutheesing (Kutub, India). A feast for women of Indian beauty-treatment and its background.

INDIAN GODS AND KINGS, by Emma Hawkridge: (Houghton Mifflin Co., New York, and the Riverside Press, Cambridge, 1935).
In this book the fabulous events of Indian history and legend, the characters of the deities, are studied in an almost biographical manner, with sympathy, accuracy and humour.

LES CIVILISATIONS DE L'INDE, by Dr. Gustave le Bon, 1887.
A rare volume illustrated with exquisite engravings, rivalling photographs in their accuracy and clarity.

GANESA, A MONOGRAPH ON THE ELEPHANT-FACED GOD, by Alice Getty.

MOORE'S HINDU PANTHEON.
First published in the late eighteenth century, this book is now a collector's piece of historical interest: but it still has to be referred to, no Pantheon containing such a collection of material having been assembled since. It is illustrated with rather naïve line-drawings.

JOHN MURRAY'S HANDBOOK OF INDIA, BURMA AND CEYLON.
This useful little volume combines facts of historical, artistic and geographical interest, splendid maps and much practical information. How to get to Mohenjo-daro, for example, and how to find the right things to see when you get there, and where to stay *en route*; invaluable to the traveller, and delightful for those confined to the arm-chair excursion.

L'INDE, by Rene Grousset. (Librairie Plon, Paris.)
A recent publication, with outstandingly beautiful photographs of many kinds of Indian art—worth having even if you don't understand French. The text is, of course, splendid as well.

INDEX

No. 79911

Form C.L.—D.

Renfrew County Library.

The entries on this label must not be in any way interfered with.
The Book should be returned on or before the latest date entered below.

2 5 JUN		
2 3 AUG		
5 AUG		
11 NOV		
1 - DEC		
- 4 JAN		
2 Z MAR		

FRIVOLOUS FINALE:
The "Fakers" in action

Some of the many splendid dance-critics of India have been mentioned in this book, also some of the pioneers of the West who championed Indian art and thought; they paved the way for the present and welcome renaissance of the dances of India, which so narrowly and so recently escaped complete oblivion.

Unfortunately the picture of Indian dancing to-day would be incomplete without some reference to the less impressive side of Indian dance-criticism—the "Fakers", semi-humorous, semi-dangerous pseudo-critics who always try to attach themselves to any popular dance-form. So here they are: Sri Bhubbal of the East, and Madame Zqueak of the West, with an airline ticket apiece, out to "do Indian dancing" in the shortest possible time.